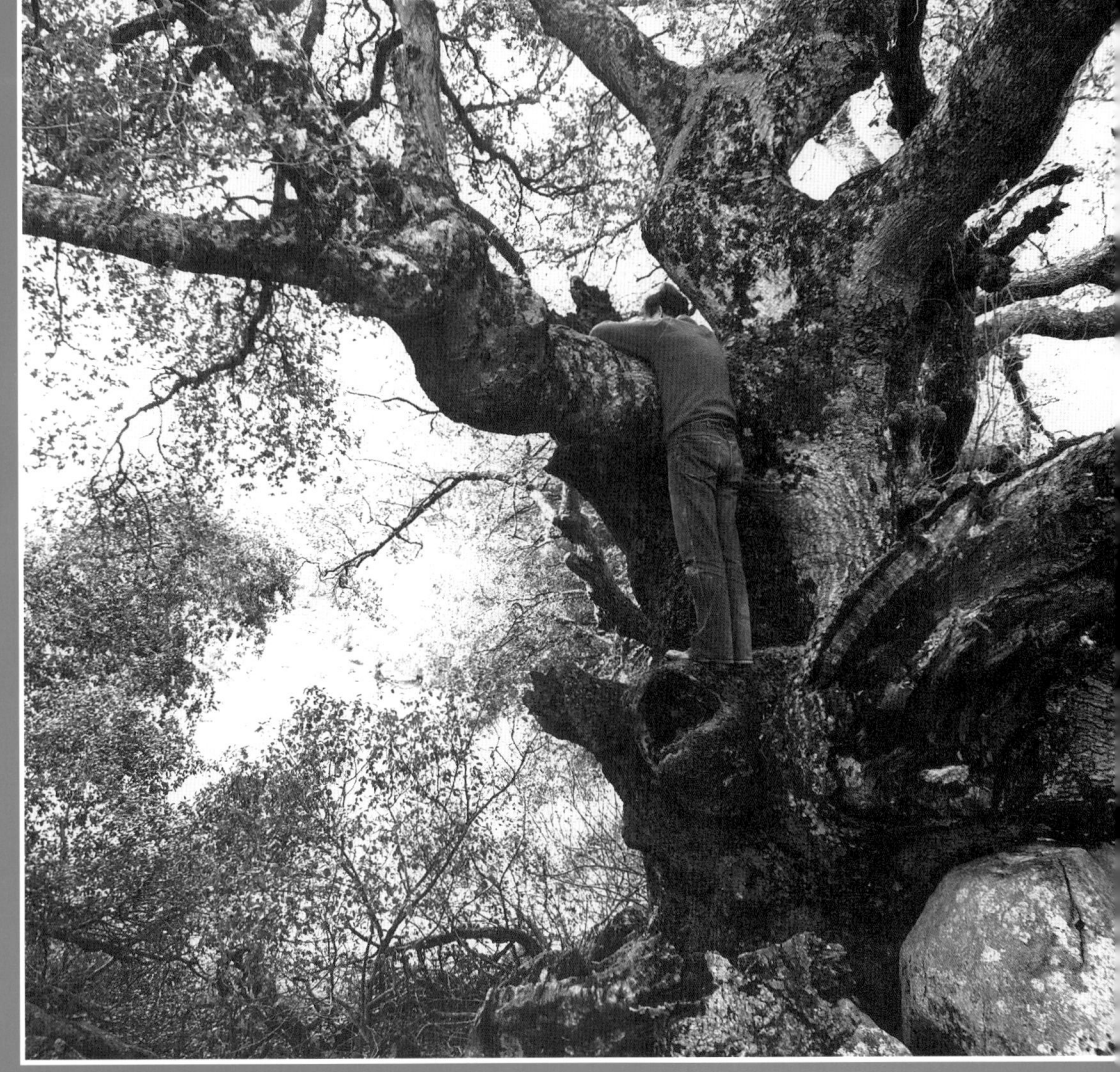

My heart is a palace

My mind is a meadow

My home is a cloud

My life is a dream

for you.

James
HUBBELL
Retrospective

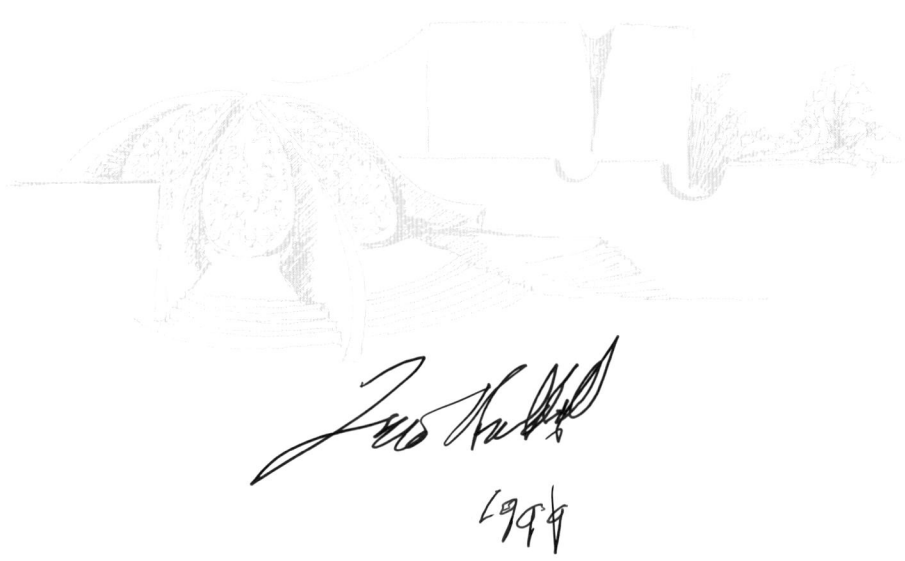

JANUARY 24 — APRIL 12, 1998

An Exhibition of the Oceanside Museum of Art

CURATOR'S STATEMENT

When planning the inaugural year of the Oceanside Museum of Art, the exhibition committee early recognized the importance of being the venue for the first retrospective exhibition of James Hubbell. Because of the architectural significance of the museum building, designed by Irving Gill in 1934 as the Oceanside City Hall, we believed that focusing on the work of a contemporary local architectural designer and artist would form a logical bridge between its early history and its present use. And because Hubbell's work has never been limited to one medium, or one mode of expression, the exhibition would be wonderfully diverse and richly rewarding. The next step was pursuading James that this was indeed a great idea. Asking an artist to pause to take the time for the retrospection, introspection, and plain hard work necessary for such an exhibition is asking a great deal. Particularly so in the case of James Hubbell, whose astonishing schedule may at any one time include public and private architectural commissions, stained glass, sculpture, drawings, paintings, and jewelry, not to mention lectures, work with architecture students, and projects around the world, and writing which most often expresses itself as poetry.

We are indebted to his assistants, architectural designer Kyle Bergman and artisan Cher Brown for their endless hours of research and cataloging of the various pieces in the show, to Otto Rigan for his help in identifying which would be most historically significant, and to those collectors willing to loan cherished objects to the Museum for more than two months. I am especially grateful to Kay Kaiser for her willingness to consult with me about so many aspects along the way, and to Robert Perine for his splendid job of designing this catalog.

I also owe special thanks to the Museum Board for its unstinting support for the exhibition and particularly to board members Darrell Dixon, Bobbie Thill, and George Schleder, and exhibition committee member Trish Williamson, for their instant recognition of the importance of this catalog, and to the sponsors and patrons without whose generous financial support the catalog would not have been possible.

—*Peggy Jacobs*

CONTENTS

Curator's Statement
Peggy Jacobs **3**

Unity and Diversity
Otto Rigan **5**

Nature at the Core
Kay Kaiser **17**

Ilan Lael Foundation **27**

Time Line **44**

Books and
Periodicals **47**

ARTIST'S ACKNOWLEDGEMENT

The work that I have been able to accomplish would not have been possible without the help of my many dedicated and talented studio assistants, the trust and enthusiasm of my clients, and the hundreds of hours volunteers and friends have so generously given. Thank you.

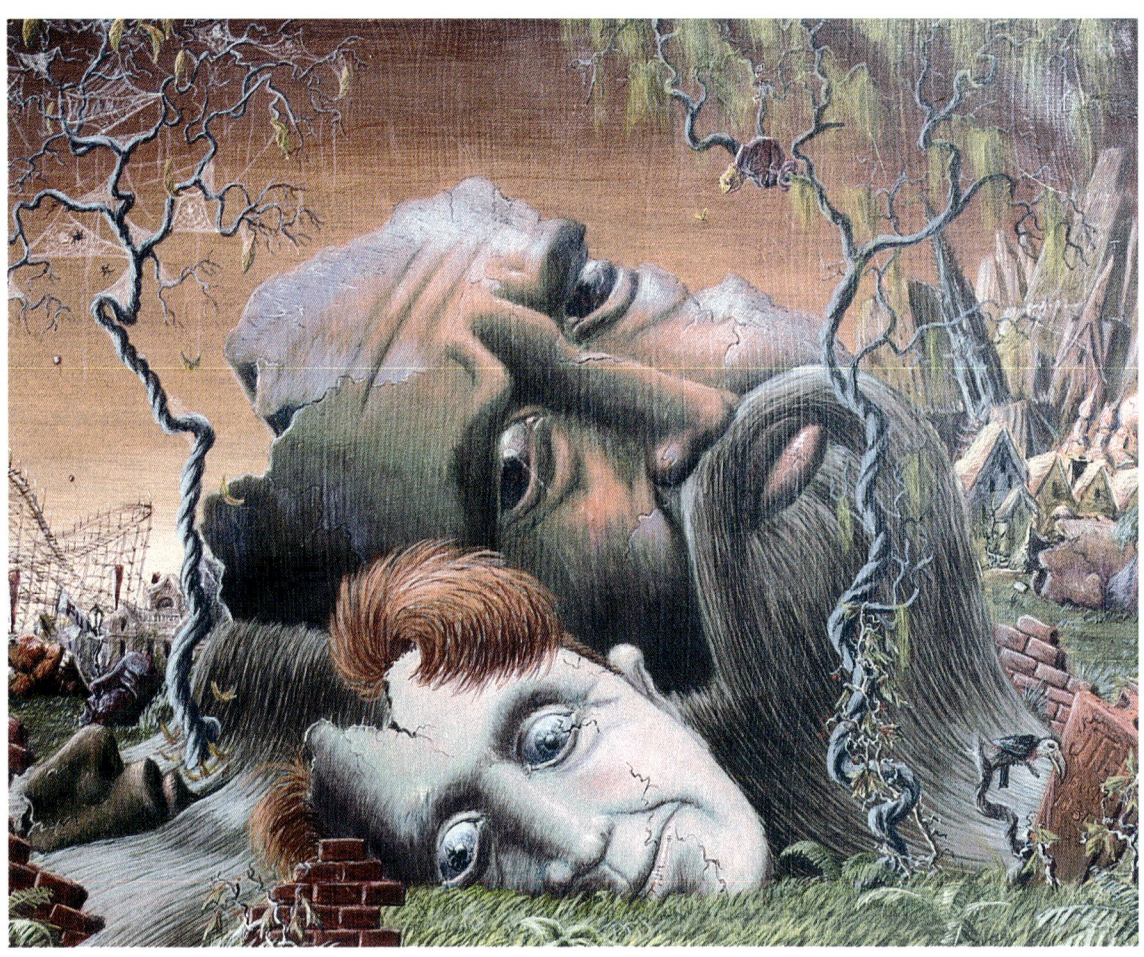

"Self-portrait," Whitney Art School, egg tempera, 20" x 12 ½", 1952.

Algerian sweeper in a small town in the Pyrenees. Pen and ink, 1951.
Right: **Native girl,** Kaoko Veld, Southwest Africa. Pen and ink, 1951.

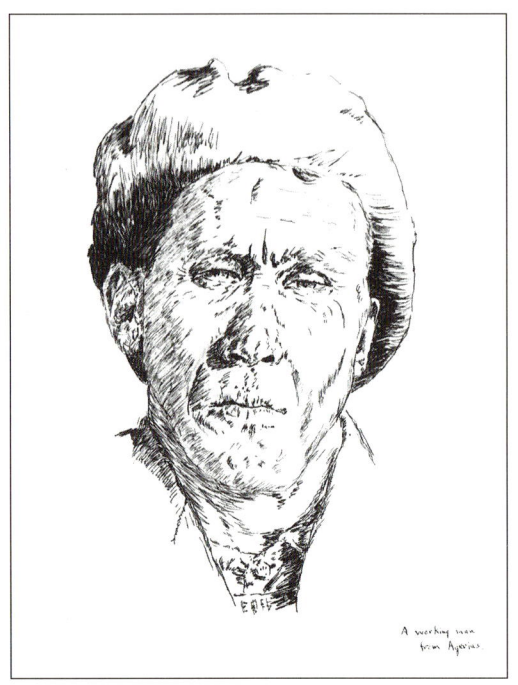

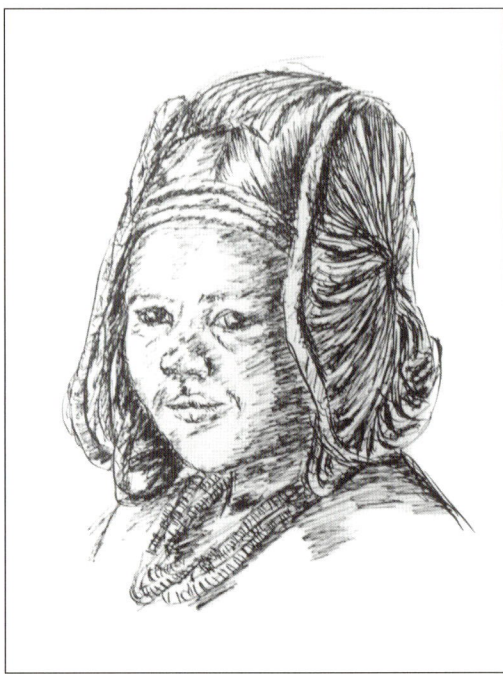

UNITY AND DIVERSITY

Otto Rigan

One cannot look at any part of James Hubbell's vast output without connecting a singular work with every other, no matter the medium. Whether a watercolor, a panel of stained glass, or sculpture, the linkages are quite apparent. We might call this phenomenon "the pattern that connects," and consider it central to appreciating all that James Hubbell has accomplished. This connecting is an intermingling of the artist's life and work, a seamless melding of experience, philosophical perspective, and reverence for nature . . . combined with his conscious inclination as an artist to turn his convictions into a unique, ongoing body of diversified works.

IN ONE'S TIME

In Hubbell's art is found a direct interpretation of his life and experiences. It is as if the acts of making and creating are beholden to these experiences. For Hubbell the process is cumulative, not exclusive. Editing is not his method. Inclusion is.

On two of his earliest overseas pilgrimages, the young James Hubbell traveled through Europe, including Spain, France, and parts of Africa. These trips, like others to follow, are evident—even thematic—in his art today. In Spain he happened upon the organic architecture—and broad palette—of Antonio Gaudi, whose influence is undeniably present in Hubbell's richly textured, organomorphic sculpture and architecture. In Paris, the inspiring forms (flying buttresses and soaring arcades) and reverence-eliciting nature of Notre Dame can be seen in his often-expressed allusion to the spiritual. His inclination to develop a community around any sizable project is not unlike the manner in which medieval communities collaborated in building their cathedrals. Medieval architecture also introduced Hubbell to the dynamics of light and color as seen through stained glass, a medium he continues to experiment with today. In Africa he encoun-

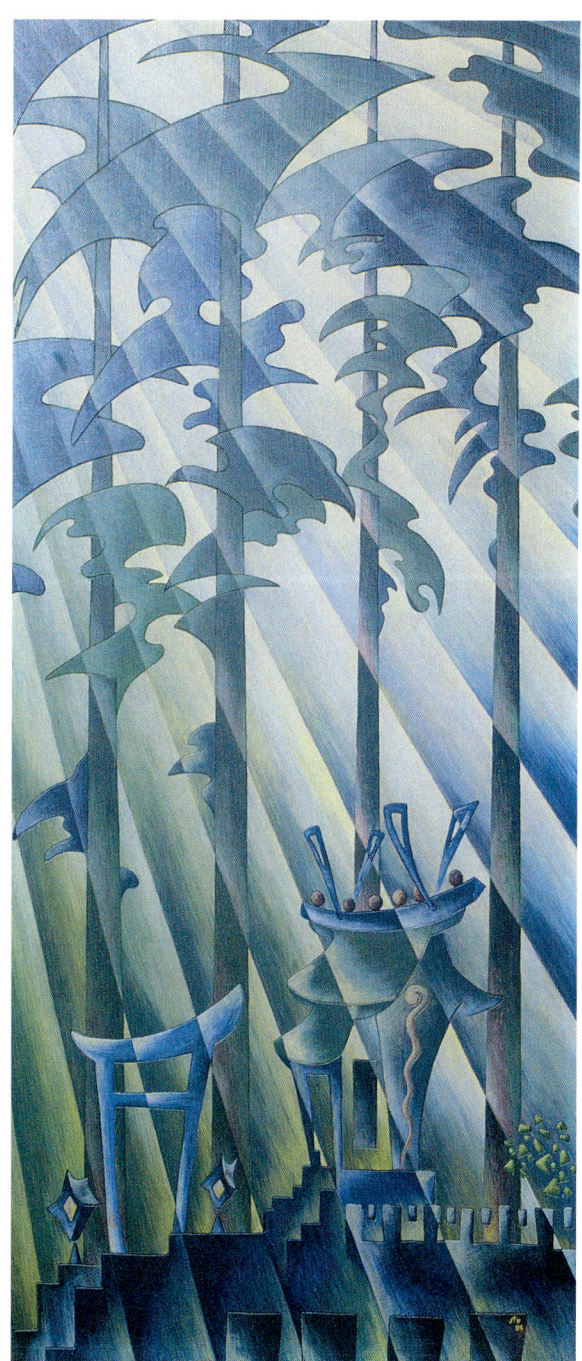

"Japanese Shrine," egg tempera on gesso panel, 30" x 15½ ", 1954.

"A mistake, like a weed, is a flower we have not learned to value."

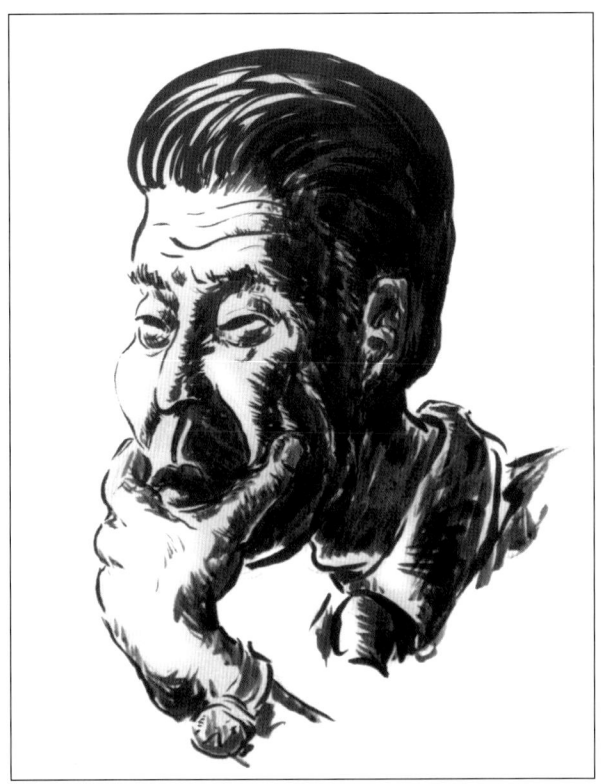

Korean house boy, Taegu, Korea. Brush and ink, 1954.

forewerd to it with expectations.
While I was home I had watched the
Rebuplican convention It was certainly fasinating
and I was pleased with the result. a few times
some of Mothers friend came to dinner. and
some times I would go over to the other house
but little ealse exsitubnt happened

I have stared working on the stained glass
I had a terrible time figuring what to do. finnaly
figuring after a day of freting on a sort of like
it was all I could come up with.
It wasn't too hard cuting the glass
althongh It was a bit crude.
but find piece to fit in was like
a cross word puzzle. I had
very little glass of the right colors
leff.

Thoughts about first stained glass
window in early sketchbook, 1953.

tered cultures that blend artifact, architecture, and ritual. These experiences were fundamental to his consummate blending of media and style.

Returning to America, Hubbell studied painting at the Whitney Art School for a year before once again traveling abroad. This time his military service in the Army mandated an assignment to Korea. Even in the midst of war, however, Hubbell spent much of his time painting murals on mess hall walls. On a "rest and recuperation" leave to Japan he investigated wood block printing and lacquer painting.

Once honorably discharged, Hubbell returned again to school, this time as a sculpture student at the Cranbrook Academy in Michigan. His Whitney and Cranbrook experiences were no doubt helpful to his apprenticeship in the early years. Through these travels, then, came his major influences. Leaving Cranbrook, he returned to Europe and studied stained glass for a year before moving to southern California, the place he soon called home.

To this day, whether he takes a day trip to one of San Diego's beaches, a hike in the Sierra-Nevada mountains, or a camp out along side the Sea of Cortez, one finds evidence of these experiences in his art.

Though his travels and his studies were critical to his development, so were certain people who found their way into Hubbell's life. Three in particular come to mind who had immeasurable influence, each in a very different way:

Quentin Keynes, a distinguished English film maker and traveler, crossed paths with Hubbell while the two were visiting New York City. This meeting led to a lengthy trip to Africa where Keynes was shooting a film and Hubbell explored various cultures and painted watercolors.

While still in his early twenties, he met the prominent San Diego architect Sim Bruce Richards. It was Richards who recognized the young artist's talent and put him to work designing entry ways, columns, gardens, stained glass windows, and other architectural components for the mentor's various projects. It is hard to imagine a better way to sponsor an energetic soul, to invite that soul into such a sophisticated context. For years Richards stuck with his pupil/associate, creating for Hubbell a structure within which he could focus his energies and

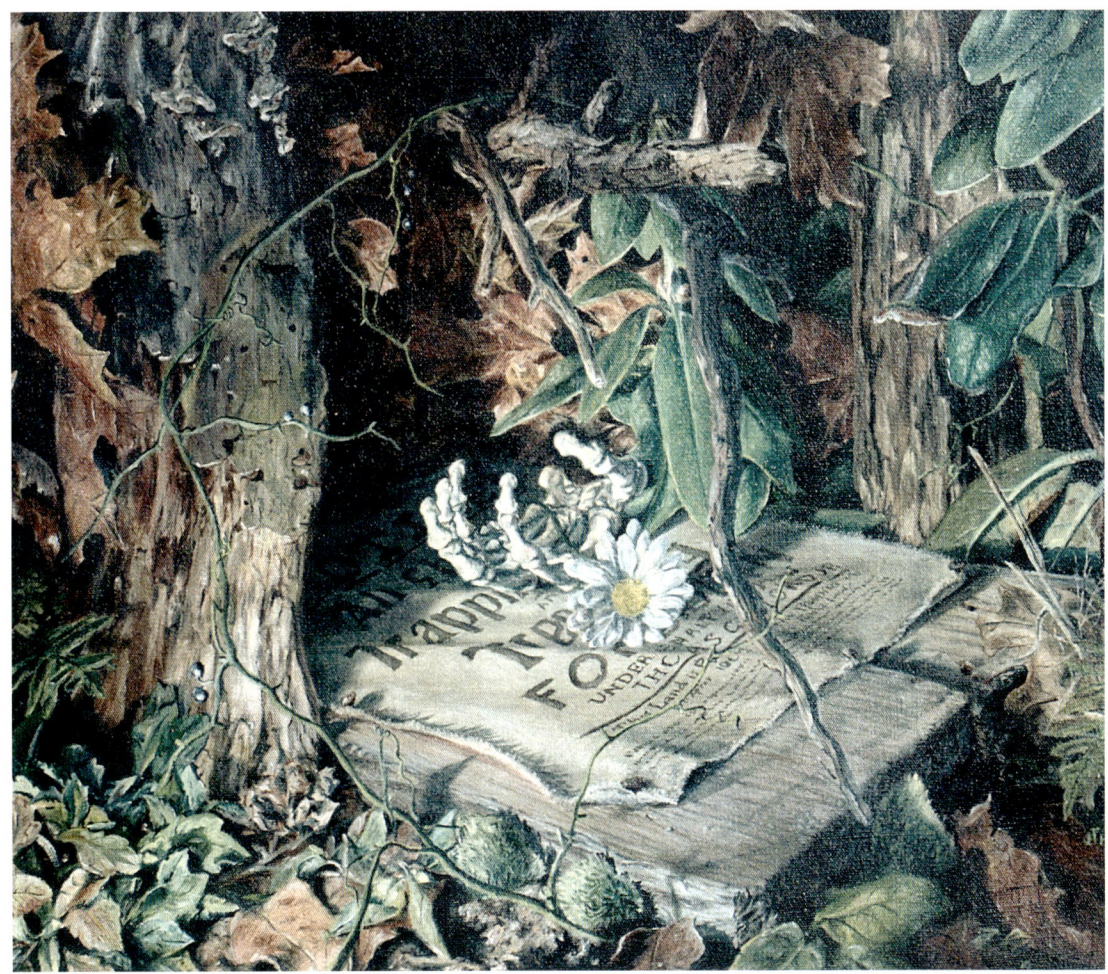
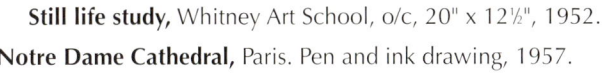

Still life study, Whitney Art School, o/c, 20" x 12½", 1952.
Notre Dame Cathedral, Paris. Pen and ink drawing, 1957.

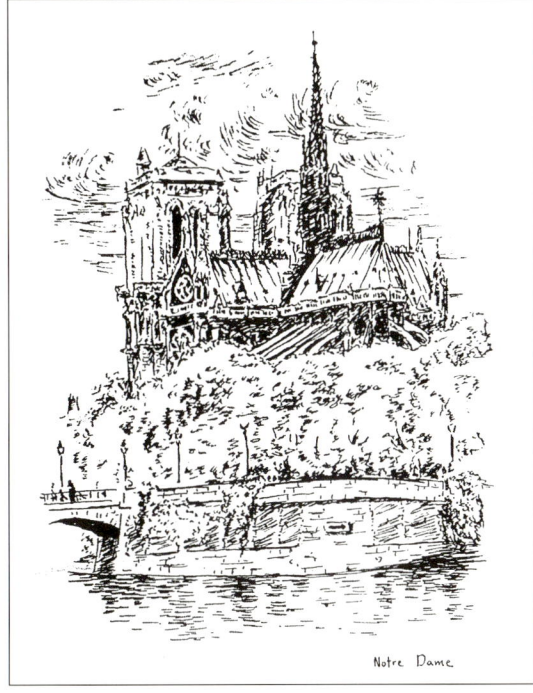

Notre Dame

"It may be that my fascination with what I call beautiful is not understandable. It may be that beauty has to do with balance, then with an Ideal Good, the pairing, the joining of Venus and Mars, the expression of the whole process of life, birth, and destruction, and back again."

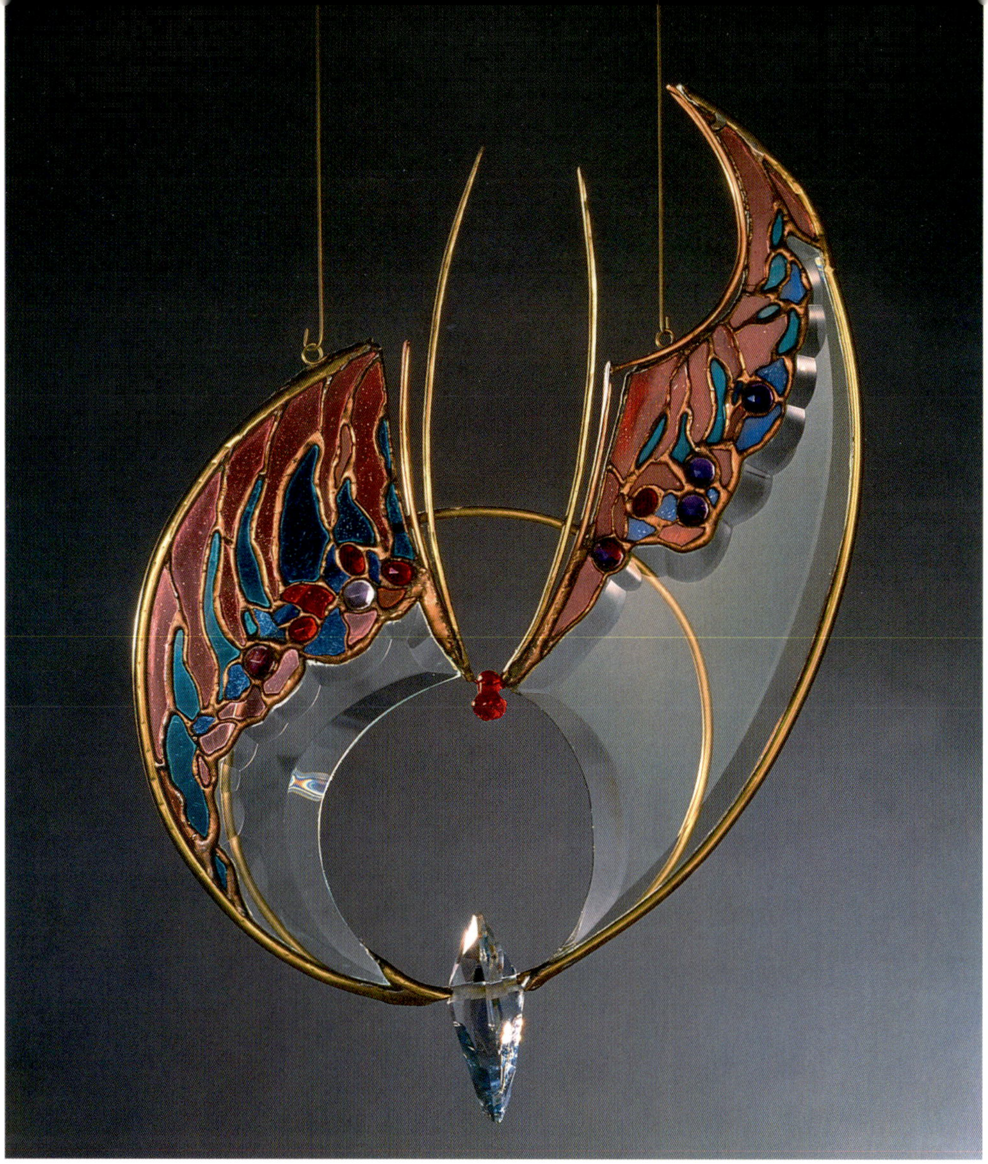

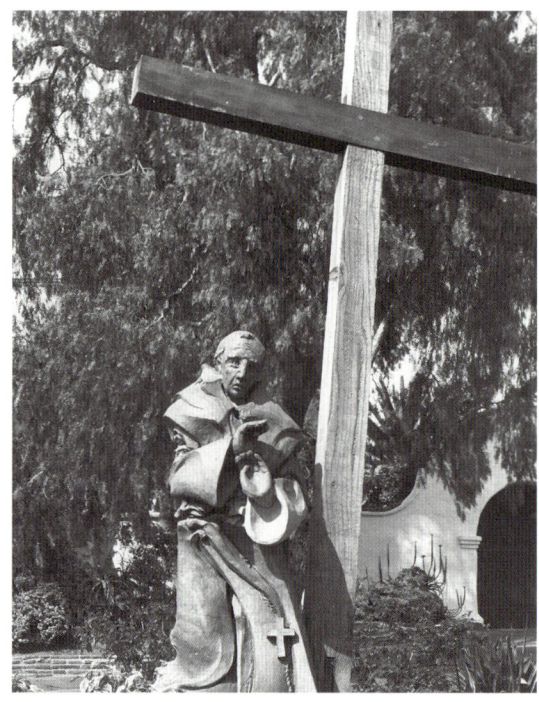

Untitled, stained glass, beveled glass, and brass, 12" x 17", 1982. (Photo by Gene Faulkner)

Below: Vista Regional Center, San Diego County Courthouse; Main entrance facade, Vista, California (San Diego County 1% for Art). Sculptured cement, tile, and carved wood, 1978.

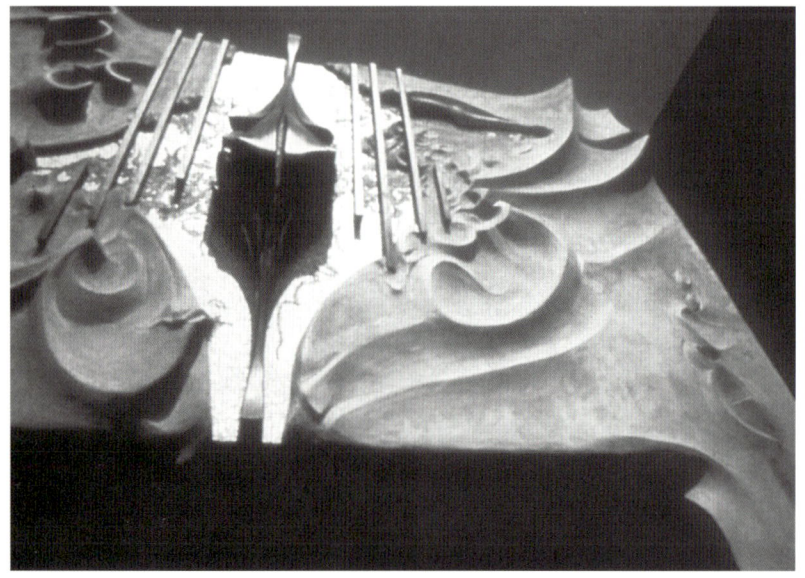

Father Junipero Serra, life size clay sculpture, San Diego Mission de Alcala, San Diego, 5' 4" tall, 1976. (Photo by Zachariah Bruce)

ideas, a place to mature and also make a living.

Finally, the effect of his courtship and marriage to Anne Stewart would be difficult to underestimate. The union catalyzed their joint and individual convictions, quickly inspiring Hubbell to design and build a home to house their growing family.

A NATURAL AESTHETIC

Nature as the moving force for art in our civilization has probably manifested itself since the first art emerged into society. The depiction of landscape has come to embody the ideas, concerns, and politics of humans, their cultures, and relationships to the natural world. As such, nature is used as a metaphor, a backdrop to artists looking for a way to relate to the rapidly changing world.

Both nature and landscape play a central role in what James Hubbell creates, but there is a different way of looking at his aesthetic. With

little exception his is an art not so much *about* landscape, but *as* landscape. Rather than illustrating or aping the landscape, the majority of his work embodies or emulates nature. As such, it is an extension of the landscape, or represents a landscape of its own. Rather than illustrating a flower, for example, he might intuitively act out the exuberance of the flower through the medium of the moment. In this sense, what Hubbell builds is all about the act of empathetically creating—not recreating—the natural *first* inspiration. This process renders the human more natural and creates a more natural world to merge with the world of the man-made.

"Art" to Hubbell is a verb, not a noun. To him, making art is not to ponder and plan, but to activate. For him, to think is to do. To do is to find. And to find reveals reason to keep looking. His process is constant, not static. He does not isolate things for study, but delves into them.

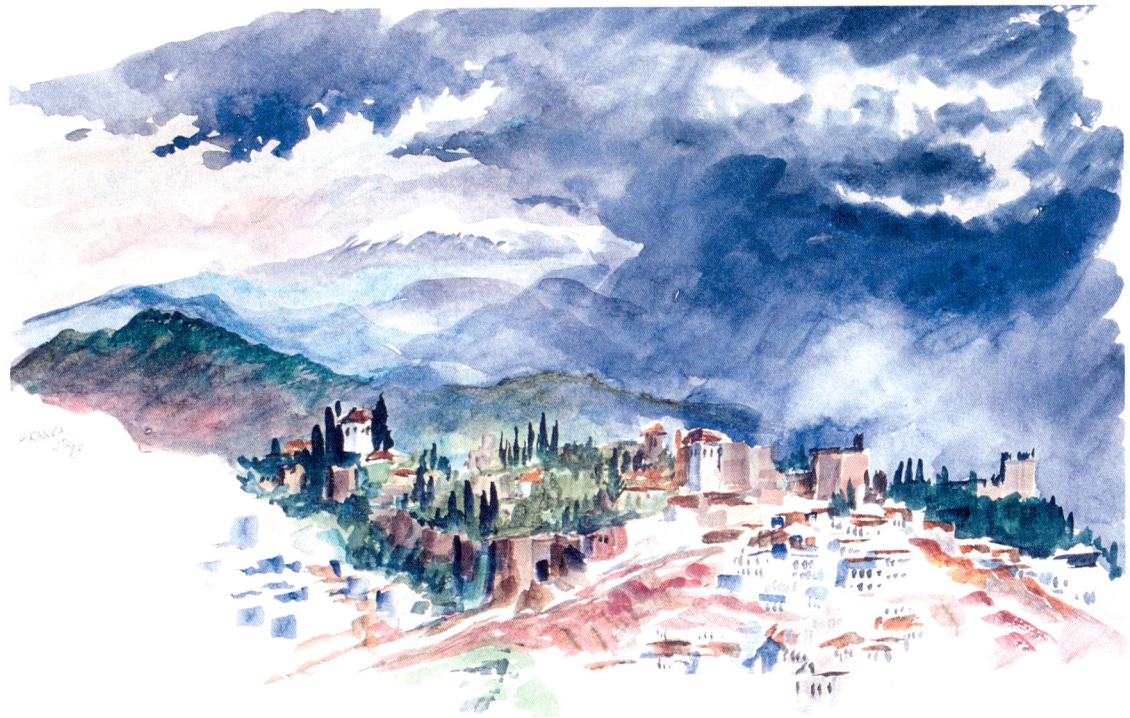

"Granada, Spain," watercolor, 11" x 15", 1985.

A SENSE OF PLACE

To say that everyone comes from somewhere is not necessarily to state the obvious. We may all come from somewhere, but few of us belong to that place. Given the increasing velocity of our culture's pace, an intimate relationship with our locus has become less and less a factor because we are moving faster. We voluntarily left our Eden with the conceit/delusion that if we move faster and quicker, more efficiently, we will actually get "there," wherever "there" is.

At the beginning of their relationship James and Anne Hubbell chose a place to build their home (their "there"). Home and place were important to them from the beginning. Without preconception, they anticipated that the house they built would be inspired by place, and that place would gain increased meaning once integrated with what was built. That they would build a home with their own hands meant the assurity of a close relationship between family, home, and land.

They found acreage on an undeveloped mountain ridge that is oriented towards the Pacific Ocean on the west, and the Anza-Borrego desert on the east. The ridge is typical California chaparral—scrub oak, manzanita, and a rich palette of wild grasses and flora. It is frequented by deer, coyotes, wild turkey, and other critters. Boulder out-croppings punctuate the rolling hills and the ridge, dividing ocean and desert eco-systems, attracting dramatic weather patterns. This is a special place, a refuge independent—but not completely detached—from the mainstream culture of urban and suburban areas. Belonging to neither, the life that the Hubbells have woven into the site remains special.

In 1959 they began by building a small shelter. The stones used for the building were gathered from the immediate vicinity, an auspi-

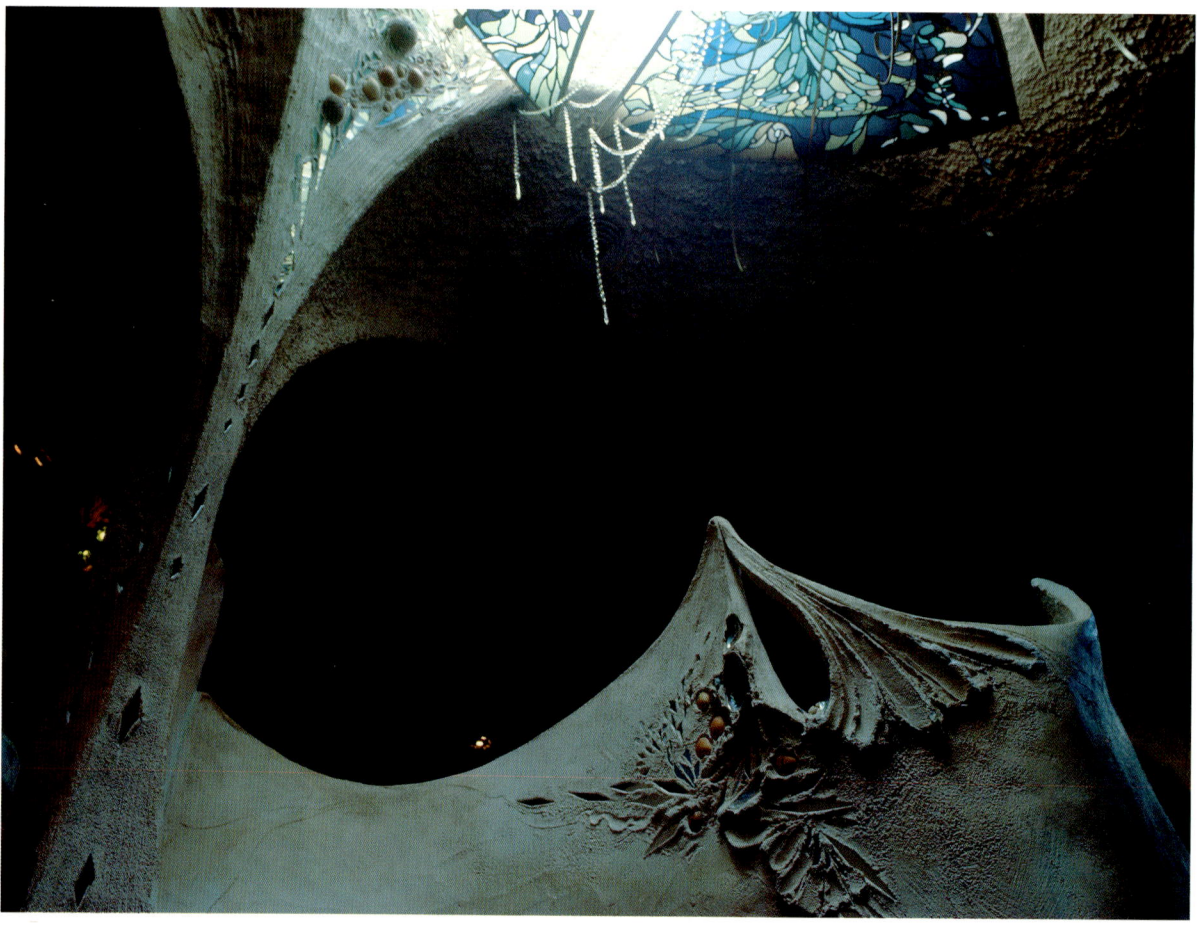

Triton Restaurant, El Cajon, California; interiors and skylight, 1975 (no longer exists)
Opposite: **Hubbell boys' house**. *(Photo by Otto Rigan)*

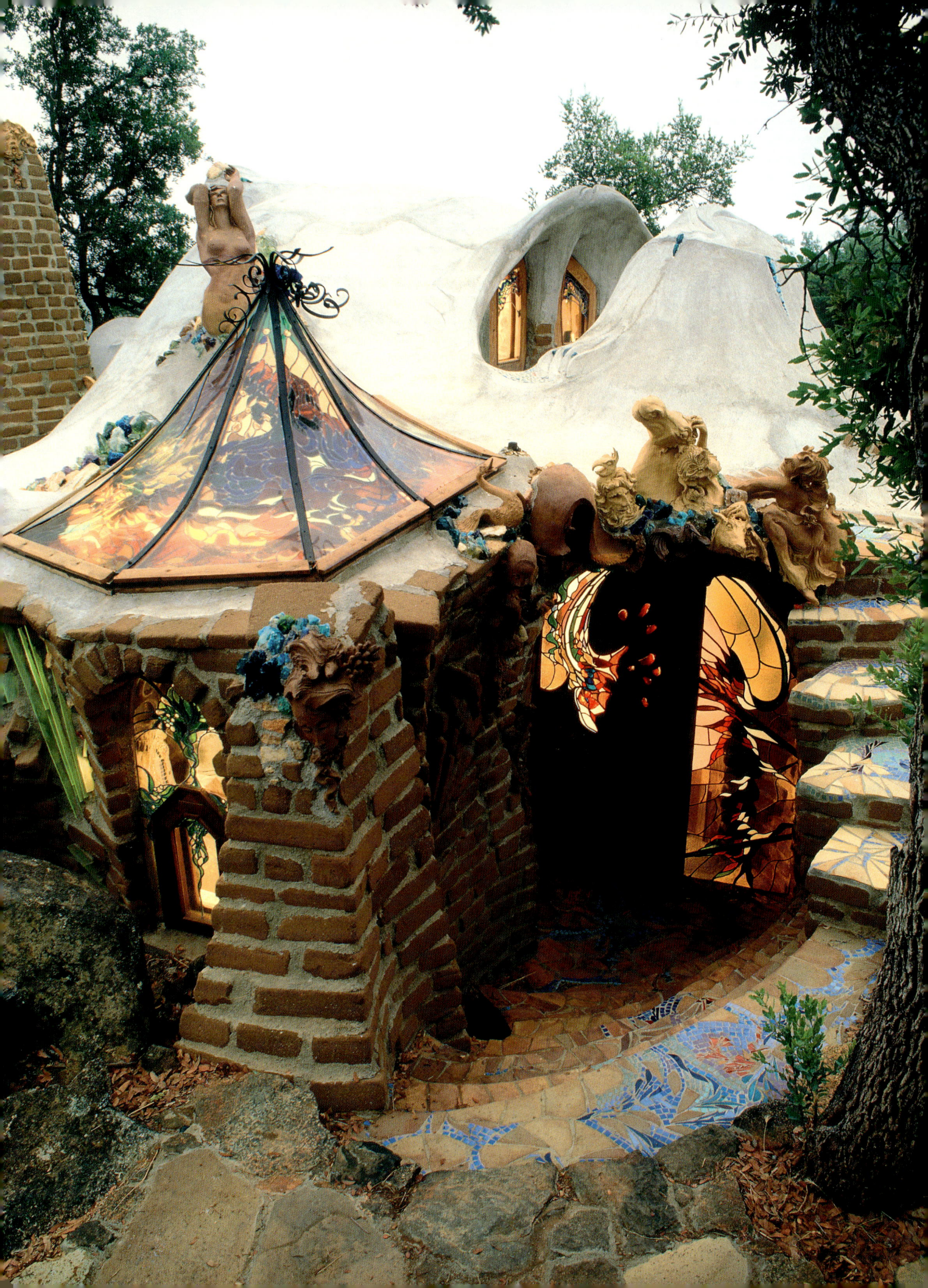

"It seems to me that the creativity in us, when shared with nature, possesses boundless energy and wants to express itself in infinite ways. That the desires driving us to "whatever level" can be looked upon as a compelling urge to unite with God, or with all else, the best of what is called Art is simply communion or worship."

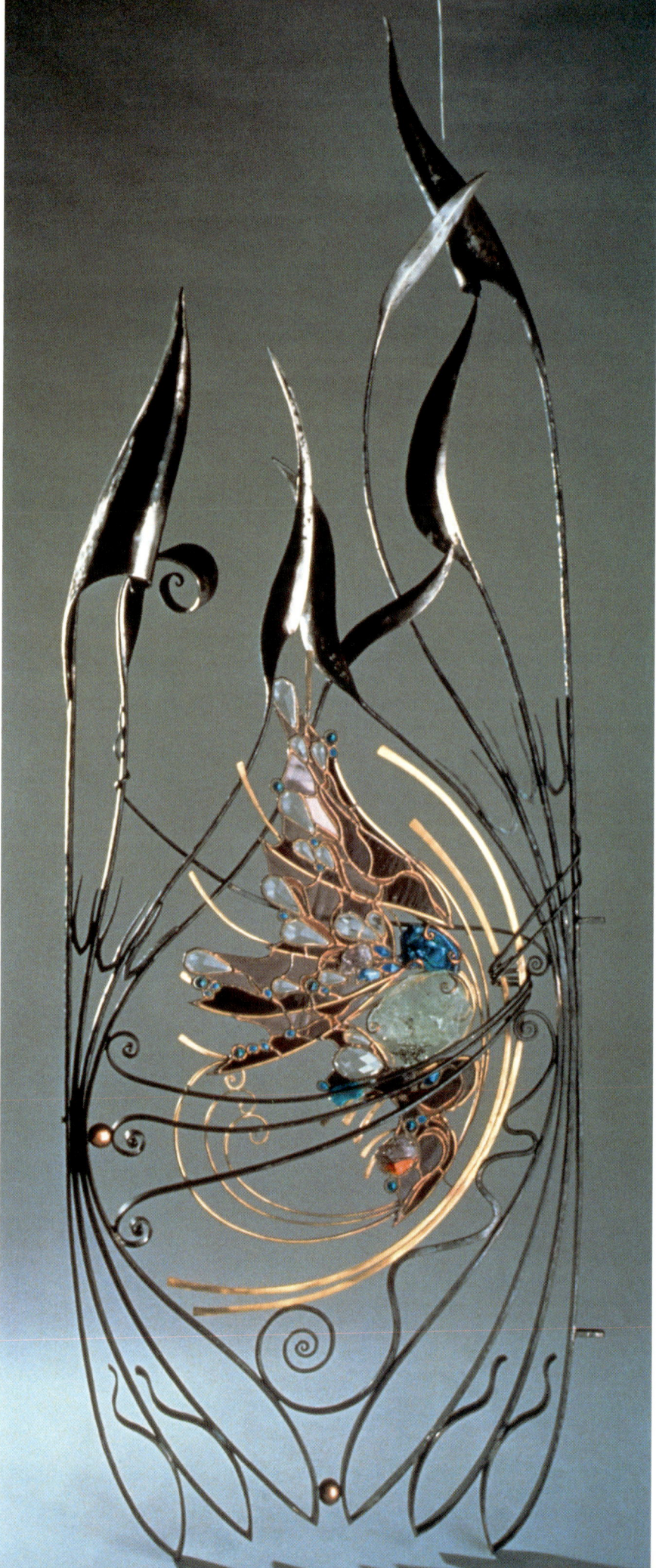

Untitled, Forged iron gate, glass, brass, forged iron, 7' 6" x 3', 1985. *(Photo by Gene Faulkner)*

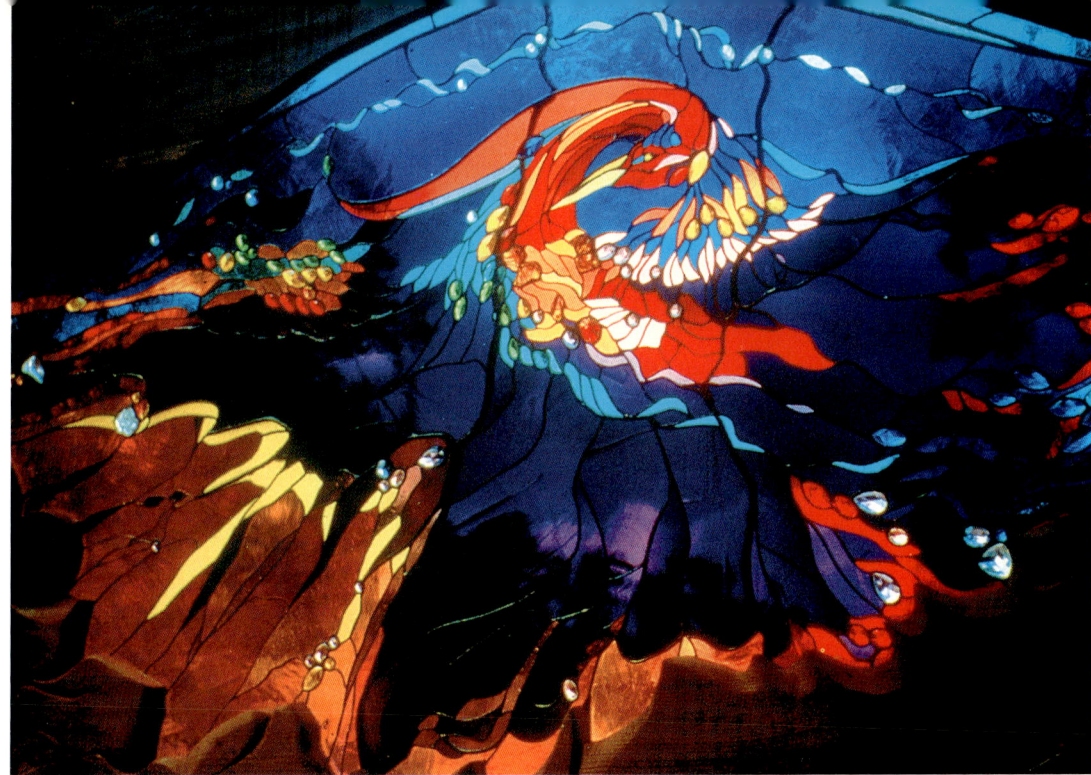

"Firebird," stained-glass window, 4' x 7', 1981.

cious start, a precedent set for all that followed. From that point on, in a tangible and measurable way, there was very little separation between the nature of the place and the architecture; between the architect and the expression of the artist; and between the family, their lifestyle, their work, and the environs.

It is impossible to imagine Hubbell's body of work as separate from the place in which it is rooted. The architectural vocabularies of Gaudi and Hubbell, for example, are no more obvious than the form and texture that the indigenous manzanita shares with his iron work, or the native flora shares with his delicate line drawings or the leaded lines in his stained glass pieces.

The place where Hubbell lives is simultaneously a nurturer, a resource, a reference, a shelter, a launch pad, and a retreat. It's also a pedestal on which, and around which, the artist continues his personal affirmation.

APART AND YET A PART

Like the location of his home, Hubbell's position as an artist is neither apart from nor a part of the mainstream Art world. "Outsider," "Eccentric," and "Naif," are overused labels defining artists or contrary thinkers who become intentionally marginalized by the use of such terms. None of these labels fit James Hubbell because he is fully engaged in asking the questions that dog

the contradictions of his time and place. Conversely, his robust cornucopia of works do not fit comfortably into the cool, distanced world of modernism or the posturing objectives of post modernism. As much as anyone, Hubbell has become a living art work, one of his own making.

Though the politics of the moment sometimes motivate Hubbell to take action, his chosen manner of expression is more often poetry, a way to speak from the heart, that inner person, a way to resolve personal belief and conflict, to some a radical departure from current fashion. The Soul and Earth Park in Vladivostok, Russia is a good example of this. In an attempt to build a symbolic bridge between cold war adversaries, Hubbell devised a plan for the Sister Cities of San Diego and Vladivostok to cooperate in the building of a park overlooking Vladivostok's Naval harbor. This park is not an overt expression of its political motivation. Instead, it celebrates pure form in an attempt to express commonality and oneness.

The method of the poet is one of process, of revealing, discovering . . . of magic. The poetic mind allows for contradiction, for paradox, for inclusion, and for inspiration. In this realm beauty and chaos coexist, each flavoring the other. Process for the poet encompasses a whole range of possibility, even reverie and contemporary myth.

It is for these reasons that defining James Hubbell is more than difficult. Conventional art/historical and art/critical writing has fallen

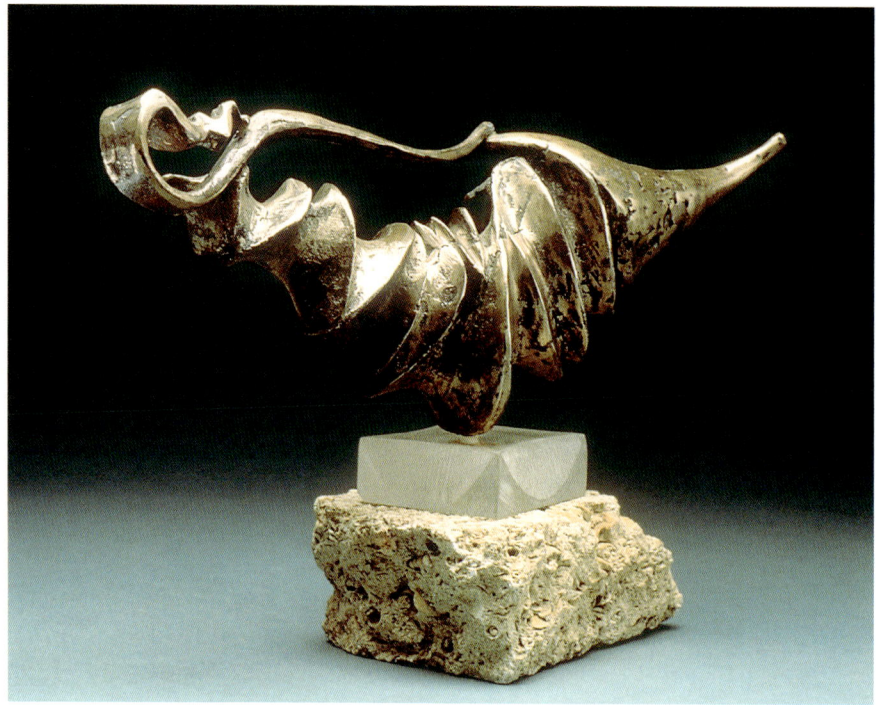

"Untitled,"
cast bronze,
Plexiglas, and
limestone, 1981
*(Photo by Gene
Faulkner)*

short of finding his essence, in large part because such systems tend to evaluate the pieces and not the whole, comparing them with peer work or current fashion in order to find a label and a slot. The best way to experience Hubbell's enormous energy is to discard convention, reconnect one's head to one's body, and receive the work for what it is in its poetic difference.

James Hubbell, in his distinctive and idiosyncratic way, is constructing a monolithic, all-inclusive artistic expression that has become a vast amalgam of poetry, architecture, family life, civic concern, and aesthetic philosophy, all as obvious to the eye and heart as nature itself. Like the bricks in one of his amorphic, close to the ground structures, the milestones in his life have fused into a discernible body of work that hints at universality of purpose . . . appealing, and uniquely his own. Short of living in one of his concrete and stone cocoons, this retrospective exhibition seems an appropriate and timely way to celebrate his vision of eclectic fusion.

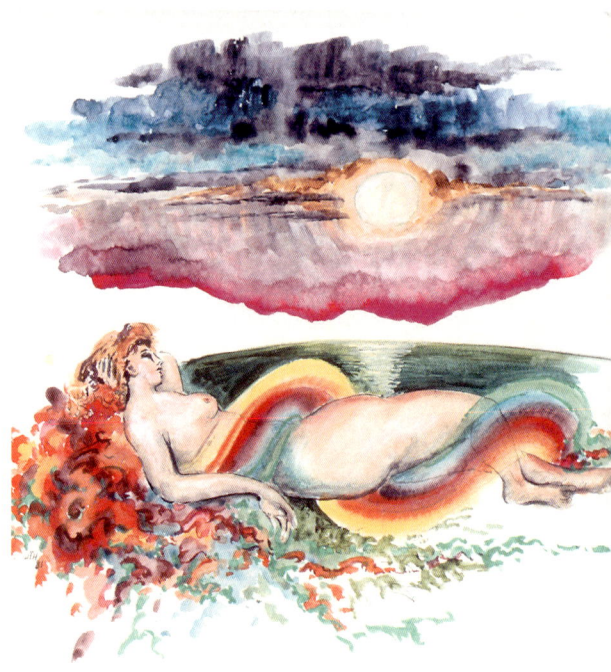

"The Pacific Ocean," watercolor, 10½" x 9½", 1981.

Otto Rigan is the author of "New Glass," and two books on James Hubbell; "From the Earth Up," and "Palace Doors of Abu Dhabi." He is a sculptor residing in Phoenix, Arizona.

Entrance door, one of eighteen doors for a palace in Abu Dhabi, United Arab Emirites. Sheet and cast bronze, beveled and leaded glass, 1982. *(Photo by Otto Rigan)*

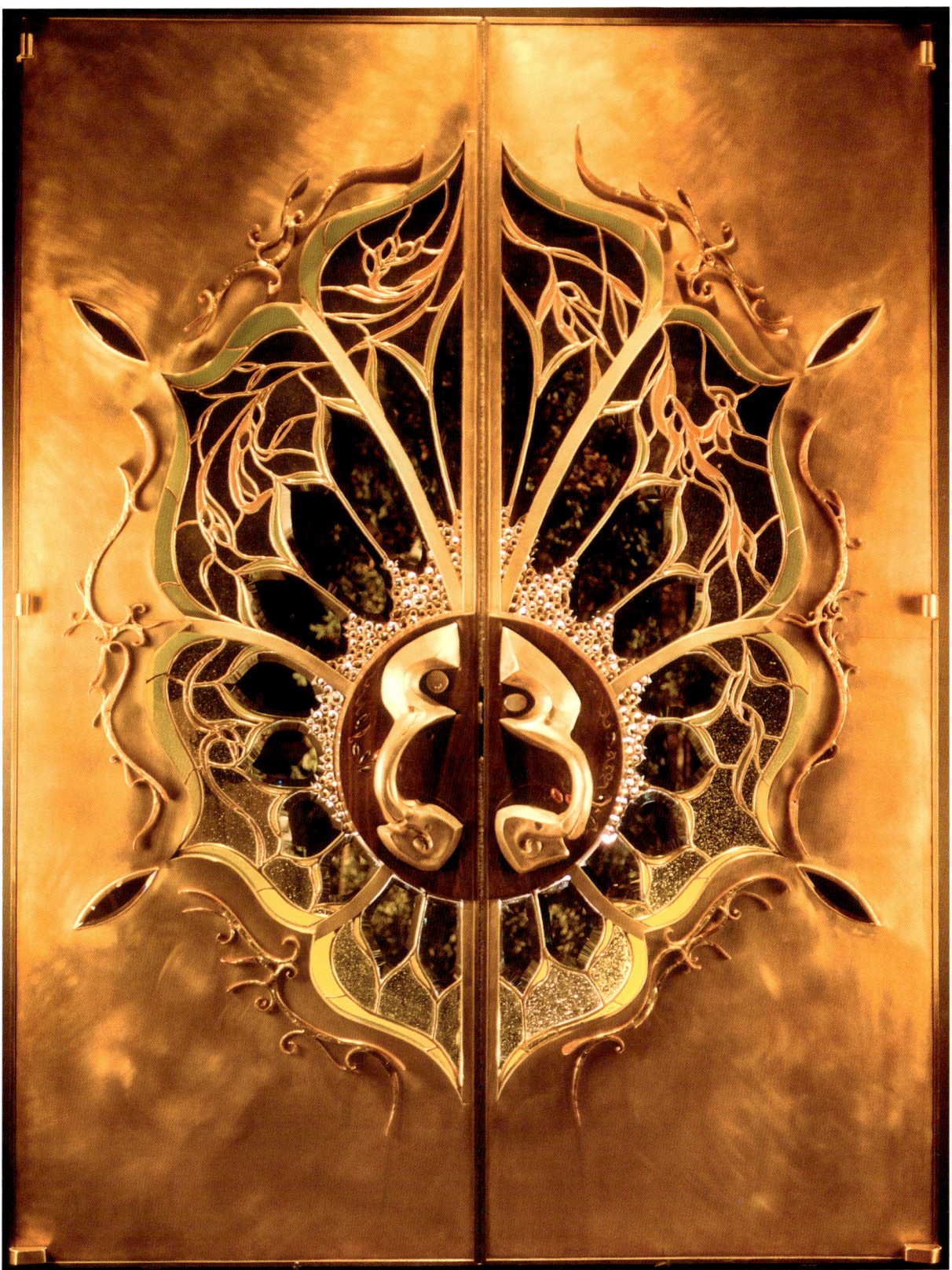

La Jolla Guest House, La Jolla, California, 1990. *(Photo by Jerry Rife)*

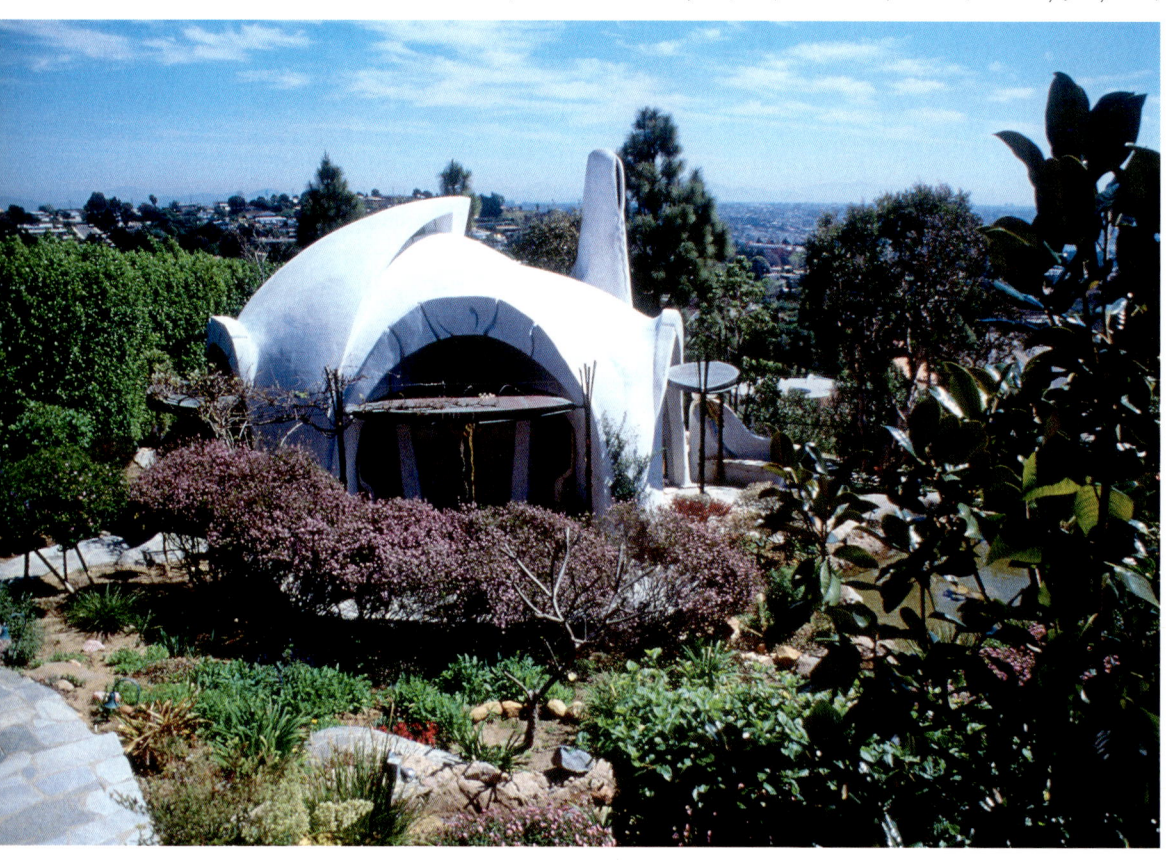

Vint Residence, Del Mar, California. Air-foam, monolithic dome, 1984.

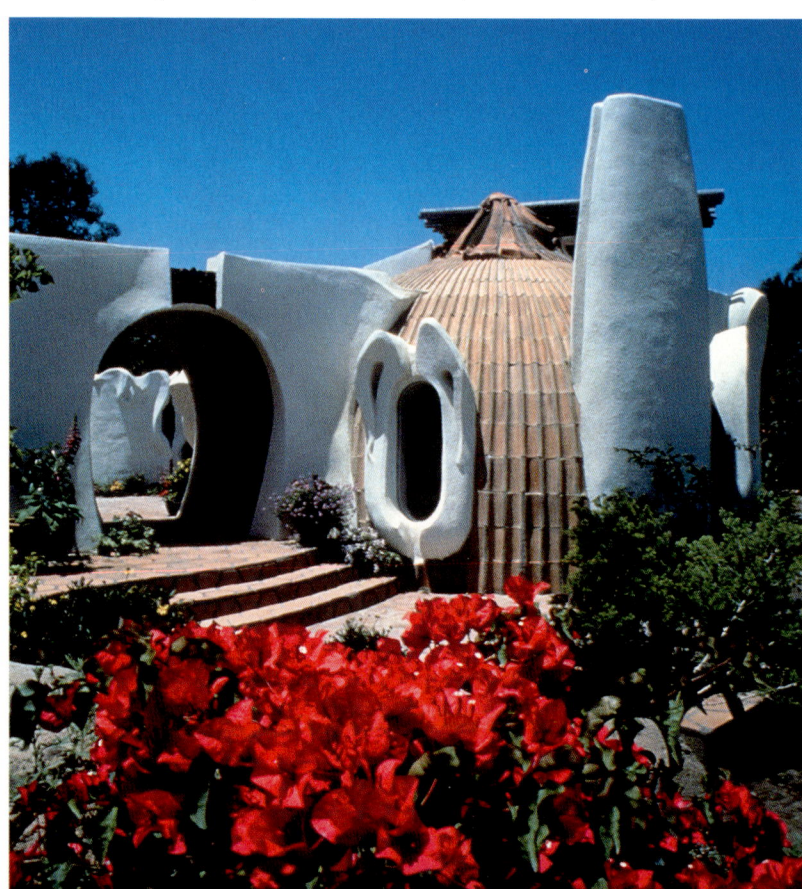

"What would architecture be like that felt like the music of Mozart?"

NATURE AT THE CORE

Kay Kaiser

"Well, I knew something would happen, but I wasn't exactly sure what," James Hubbell said while trying to explain a phenomenon, photographed for the cover of this catalog, that his clients call the "underwater watercolor." It appears only at night on the curving and segmented ceiling of their guest house.

The statement is pure Hubbell. He likes to make people think he isn't in complete control of everything that happens with his art and architecture. "If I pretend that I'm not really all there in the head, the clients ask fewer questions," he says while smiling shyly. He's joking. He listens to every word from the client and more importantly, he pays attention to what they don't say.

There are reasons for Hubbell's reticence to explain what he does. Words do not come easily to him in any situation, and he would much rather build than talk about it. He often dodges questions by telling clients not to worry, that things will work out, and they usually do. At times he may seem vague, as if he's waiting for a muse to emerge from behind a fern, but don't believe for a minute that Jim Hubbell doesn't have a plan. Part of that plan is to not allow the details to become rigidly set in his clients' minds, or his own. This allows for the spontaneous developments, made by accident or will, that occur during the building process. More often than not, these are the elements in his architecture that make his work so arresting.

The "underwater watercolor" is a good example of the Hubbell method. He knew that backlighting a stained glass clerestory window with lights on the outside edge of the building's second-story deck would cast a pattern over the ceilings of the building's rooms. But did he know exactly how it would flow over the curves, or that the pattern would reflect in other glass panels in the building? He's not saying, and it

doesn't matter whether he knew or not. What matters is the clients' response to this soft expressionist painting made by light reflected through colored glass. They regard it as a surprise gift from the artist that mesmerizes them for hours at a time. It's not unlike the blood pressure-lowering benefits gained from watching activities in an aquarium, only there are no fish to feed.

When you look at Hubbell's ceiling for more than a few minutes, the watery forms seem to move slightly. Was there a change in the tide or wind? Did a big fish just move through the water and sea grasses? But it's possible you haven't been looking below the surface of the sea at all. Maybe it's really the leafy roof of a forest, as described by William Henry Hudson in *Green Mansions*, one of Hubbell's favorite books: "Lying on my back and gazing up, I felt reluctant to rise and renew my ramble. For what a roof was that above my head! Roof I call it, just as the poets in their poverty sometimes

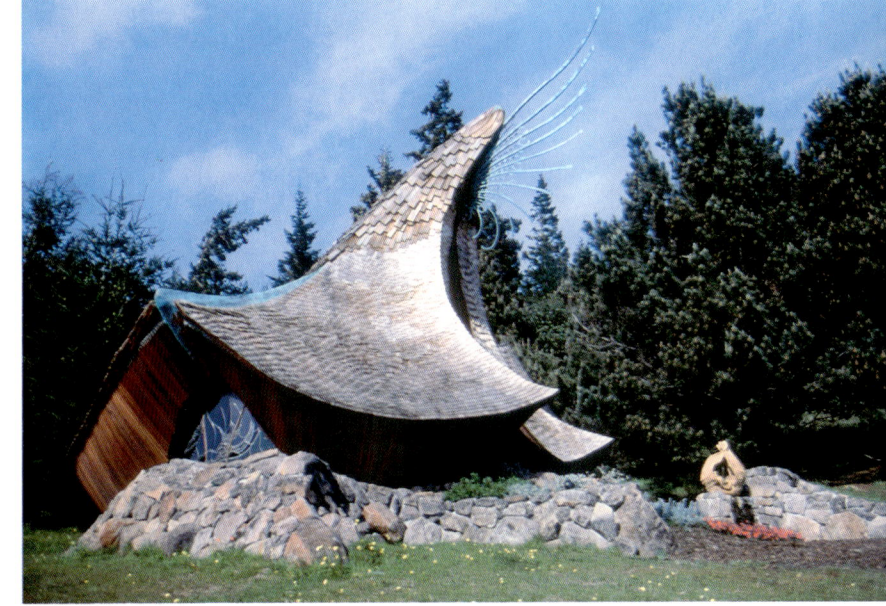

Sea Ranch Meditation Chapel, Sea Ranch, California, 1984. *(Photo by Christalen Photography)*

"If the Renaissance and Humanism represented a separation of faith and knowledge, and civilization has for the past 400 years been on a journey toward materialism, we have now reached a point in that journey which is no longer a search for heaven or an evolution from spirit to matter but an inner understanding that matter and spirit are inseparable. Dividing them destroys both."

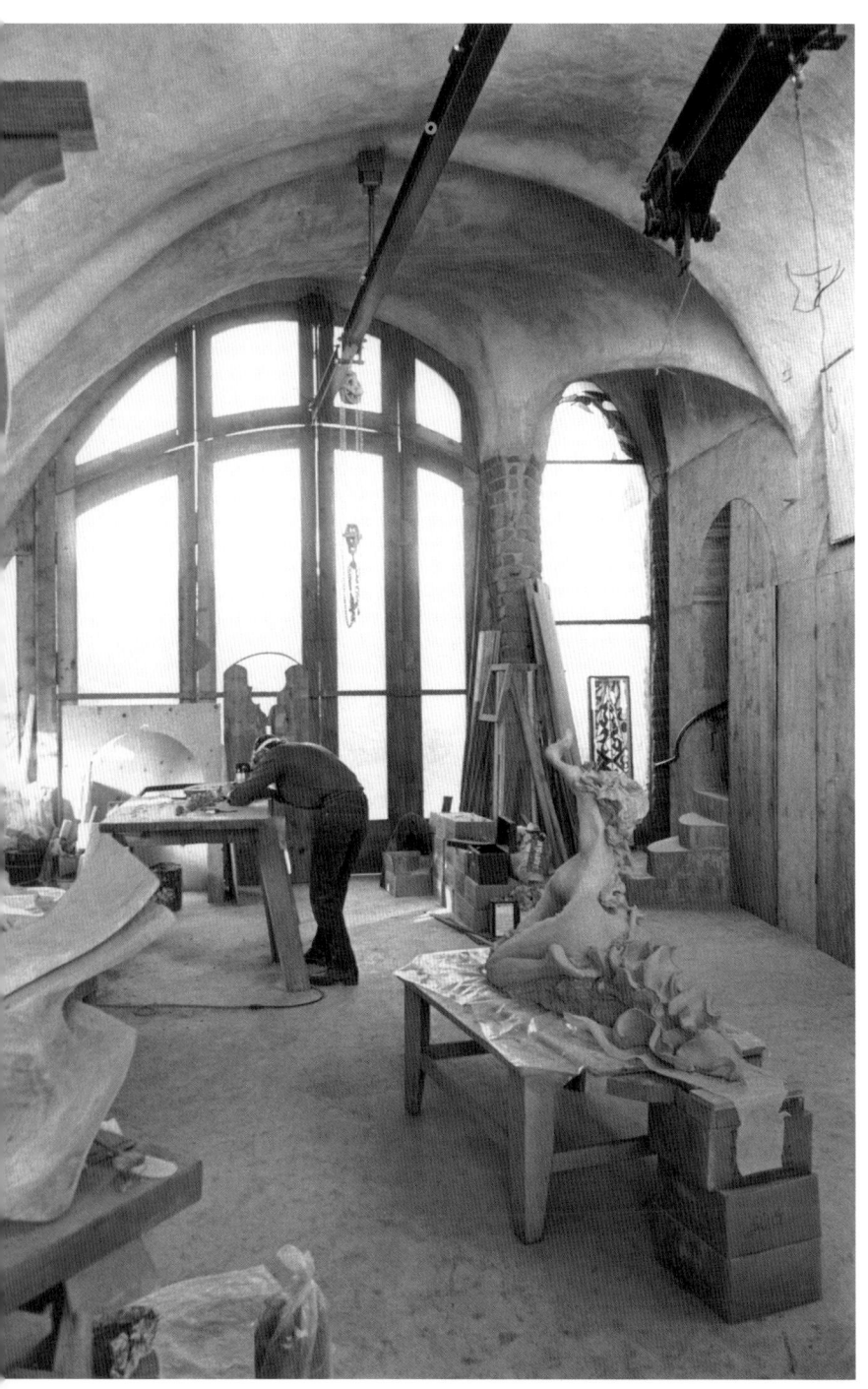

Interior of working studio, Santa Ysabel, 1980.

describe the infinite ethereal sky by that word; but it was no more roof-like and hindering to the soaring spirit than the high clouds that float in changing forms and tints, and like the foliage chasten the intolerable noonday beams. How far above me seemed that leafy cloudland into which I gazed! Nature, we know, first taught the architect to produce by long colonades the illusion of distance; but the light-excluding roof prevents him from getting the same effect above. Here Nature is unapproachable with her green, airy canopy, a sun-impregnated cloud—cloud above cloud; and though the highest may be unreached by the eye, the beams yet filter through *illuming* the wide spaces beneath—chamber succeeded by chamber, each with its own special lights and shadows."

But then again, could this luminous display really be the aurora borealis?

The confusion over which nature form Hubbell is invoking makes this ceiling phantasma more compelling. He delights in the various interpretations, and says that fish, water, the forest and the heavens are all parts of us. Perhaps that is why it feels so good to be in this small, cavelike space.

This small example of his work serves to distill Hubbell's more than four decades as an artist-building designer. The garden building contains the luminous stained glass in doors and windows for which he is best known. The curves of the building forms are not unlike the voluptuous contours found in his drawings and sculptures of women. View the chimney from the deck, and the imagery in Georgia O'Keefe's flower paintings comes to mind. The iron columns supporting the canopy over the entrances twist and curl in patterns surprisingly similar to the wisteria that grows above them.

Nature has always been at the core of Hubbell's work. He responds to the same forces,

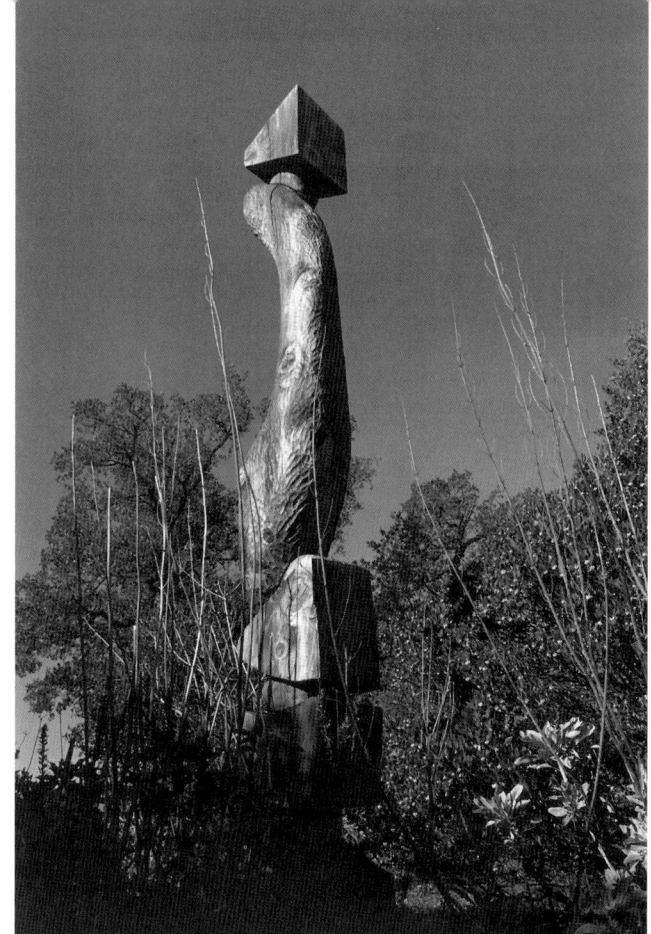

Carved cedar column, Santa
Ysabel, 10' x 14" x 12", 1964

whether he's designing a fork, a piece of jewelry, a garden gate, or a chapel. In a lecture to students at the School of Architecture in San Luis Obispo in 1965, he said he wished people could live in homes as marvelous and beautiful as that of a snail. And why, he asked, couldn't cities be as endlessly rewarding as forests?

In a lecture at the Smithsonian Institution in Washington, DC, in 1993, he compared his design process to the ways trees grow. "It begins with the earth and the seeds and where they came from and their memory, the part that the wind, light and storms play in the development of a tree," he said. "The process continues through its interaction with everything around it. In the case of a building, it also involves the people who experience it, what they contribute, what they feel or understand, and what they take away. If the builder sees the building as part of a continuous web that begins with our ancestors searching for their own shelter, identity, and myths, and continues into the realization of new form, space, and light not yet dreamed of, he or she can give the building a richness and vitality that helps carry us into a world with which we are once again connected."

With this statement, he successfully defined the way he thinks and works. These ideas came to him slowly throughout his life. He was nourished by travel to Europe, Japan and Africa. He spent a year wandering throughout Europe looking at every cathedral he could find. The attraction was the mystery and the light, but also the complexity of the structures and ornament. He was trying to discover Gothic architects' secret of how to make a multitude of design themes work together in the same building.

Hubbell's earlier background on the East Coast also contributes to his design personality. In reality, he is a taciturn Connecticut Yankee who possesses a work ethic that befits a farmer

from that region. Although he would have been a very good barn builder, Hubbell had the good fortune to see the freely expressive work of Antonio Gaudi in Spain at exactly the time he was formulating the path he would take for the next several decades. Gaudi showed him a new correlation between art and architecture, and that architecture could express the highest aspirations of the human spirit.

Hubbell credits another important influence that is less obvious than Gaudi. It is the two years he spent in 1954 and 1956 at the Cranbrook Academy of Art in Bloomfield Hills, Michigan. He went there at age 23, to study bronze sculpture, but a greater lesson came from the campus environment itself.

Cranbrook was designed in the late 1920's through the 1940's by Eliel Saarinen, the great Finnish architect who was also the institution's first director. The artists and craftsmen he brought to Michigan from Europe as instructors also participated in the design of the campus. The result was a carefully considered and integrated combination of sculpture, ceramics, iron work and fabric arts, all of which complimented the Saarinen architecture. It was here, simply by walking through the grounds and observing, that Hubbell learned how important the spaces between buildings could be, and how the variety of those spaces contributed to the whole. As in music, sometimes the emotion and power are in the spaces between the notes. Decades later, he admires Saarinen's decision to slowly make the transition from the wild, forested spaces to the highly ordered patterns within the clusters of buildings. The profound expressive quality of those transitions has stayed with him.

Although Saarinen died four years before Hubbell arrived at Cranbrook, so many of the master's thoughts seem to be part of his own design philosophy. He says he never read Saarinen's book, *The Search for Form: A Fundamental Approach to Art,* published in 1948, but many of the words echo through Hubbell's design life. "The plant grows from its seed," Saarinen wrote. "The characteristics of its form lie concealed in

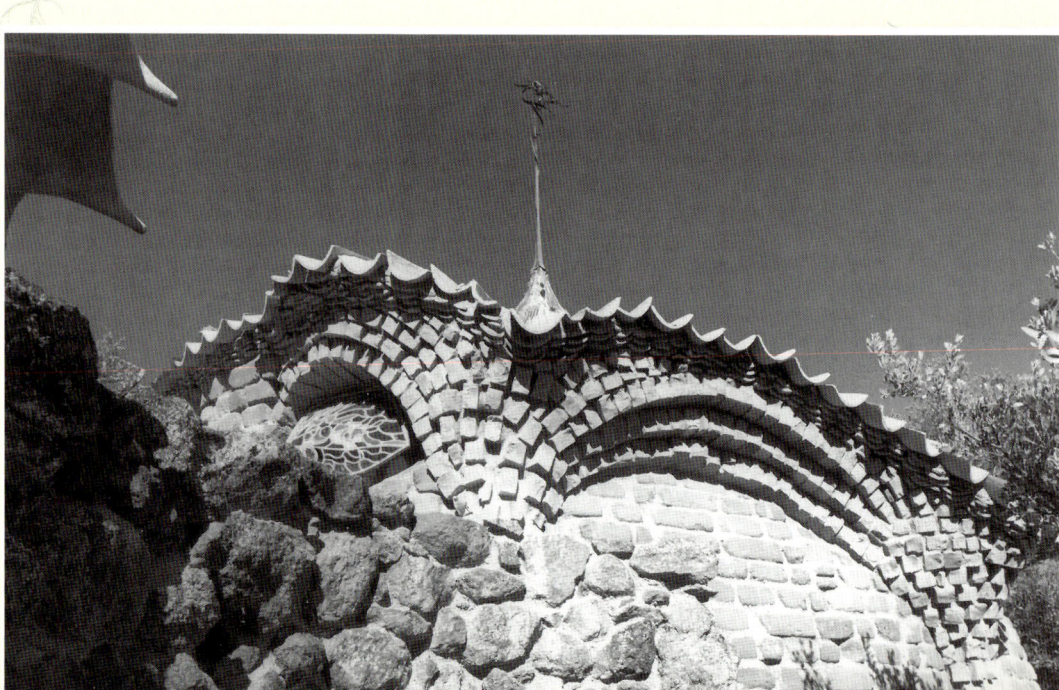

Silhouette of gallery roof and wall of Hubbell home in Santa Ysabel, 1980.

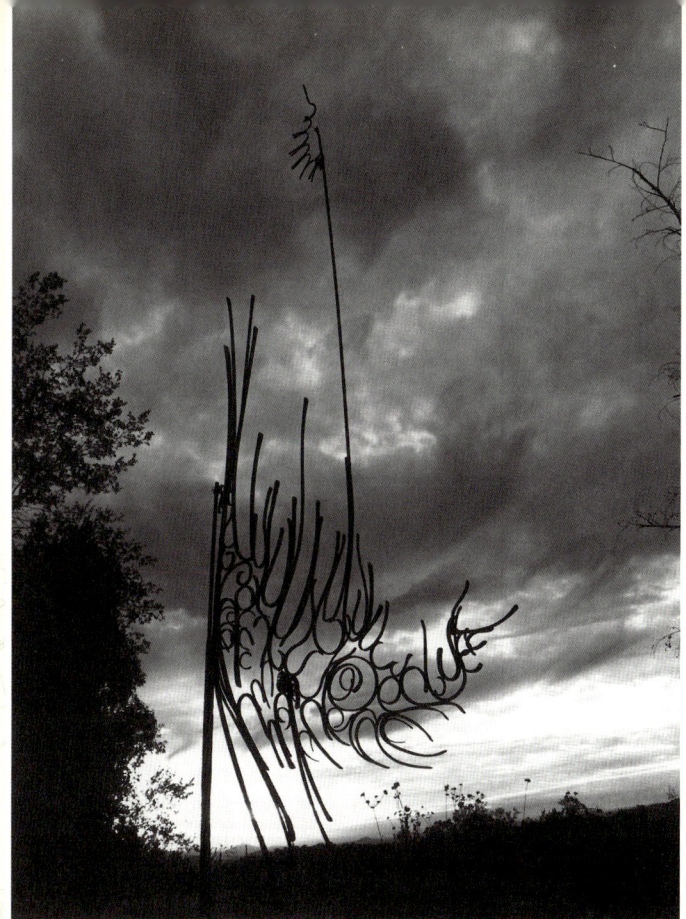

Forged iron gate at the Hubbell house. Done while at Cranbrook School. 9' x 3½', 1956.

"It often seems when working that certain problems are answered not by the brain but by what might be called the body-mind. The hands, the back of the neck tell you many things. It may be that the whole body functions as a mind and that the universe is its nervous system."

"In Memory of Dostoyevsky," bronze model; forged copper, brass, and glass. Size 24" x 24" x 9", 1984. *(Photo by Gene Faulkner)*

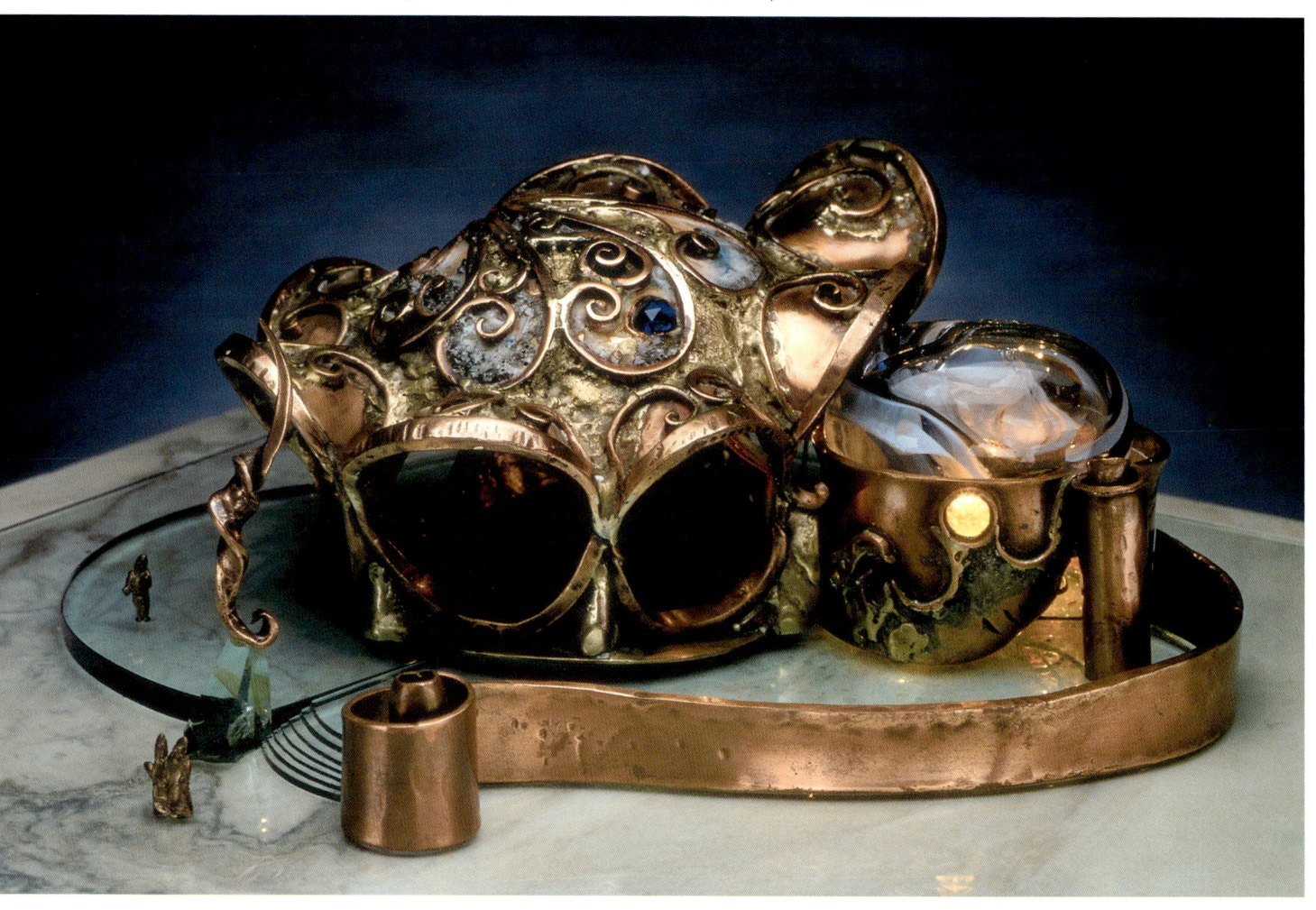

the potential power of the seed. The soil gives it strength to grow. And outer influences decide its shape in the environment.

"Art is like the plant. The quality of art lies concealed in the potential power of the people. The aim of the age is the soil that gives it vitality. And outer influences decide its fitness in the environment.

"To understand life, and to conceive form to express this life, is the great art of man."

This type of thinking about the organic nature of design must have still been in the air at Cranbrook in 1955. Hubbell breathed it in. He admits that he learns best through osmosis.

Later in the book, Saarinen defined his concept of an architect's scope of work: "During all the Great Civilizations of the past, architecture was conceived in its broadest sense. Architecture did not mean the building only: it meant the whole world of forms for man's protection and accommodation; it meant the various objects of the room as well as the room itself; it meant the building, as such, as well as the interrelation of buildings into organic groupings; and it meant the correlation of all the structural features into the complex organism of the city. Within this broad world of architectural forms, man lived and worked."

The paragraph could explain why Hubbell has always been compelled to be involved in broad city planning issues. It was obvious to him that artists and architects had a role in the design of cities. He established the Ilan-Lael Foundation primarily to make that happen. To him, San Diego's harbor, urban core, park systems, canyons and the land leading to the mountains and deserts should be like elements in a good drawing: connected, in balance and when combined, symbolic of an idea, a spirit. He also believes that it is an artist's or architect's duty to make their knowledge and vision available to city decision-makers, many of whom may have a solid grasp on business administration, but not a particularly complete understanding of the spirit of a place.

Hubbell's most important mentor in San Diego was architect Sim Bruce Richards. He died in 1983, but for more than twenty years, Hubbell made gates, doors, carved railings, lighting fixtures, rock work and many other elements for Richards's homes. Although Richards was always clearly in charge of the projects, young Hubbell just as clearly enriched Richards's work. In turn, the architect brought the beginnings of discipline to the artist's work.

As is the case with many things in Hubbell's life, Richards was exactly the right person for him to meet exactly when he did in the late 1950s. And as usual, the meeting was quite accidental. Hubbell's mother had commissioned Richards to renovate the now long demolished Wishing Well Hotel in Rancho Santa Fe. The young artist worked on many portions of the building, and the long and delightful association between Richards and Hubbell began.

Richards had been one of Frank Lloyd Wright's better students in the 1930s. He could enthrall everyone for hours with stories about life in Taliesin, Wright's schools and studios in Spring Green, Wisconsin and Scottsdale, Arizona. Between tales of Wright's eccentric relationships with clients, wives, and creditors, all of which entertained Hubbell, who is not above an occasional horse laugh at the messes people get themselves into, came lessons on the nature of materials, the importance of building in harmony with the climate and site, the dynamic power of unfolding spaces, and the pure, exuberant joy found in color and texture, and the magnificence of a shadow cast by the right tree across a rubble wall.

By observing how Richards talked with his clients, Hubbell learned that often the smallest owner concern or desire could be a big clue to their personalities and ultimately inform the total design. He recalls Richards spending an entire afternoon talking about a set of built-in drawers in someone's master bedroom closet. The old master believed it was time well spent. "I would design my clients' underwear, if they would let me," he was known to say. Yet he often threw his hat into the public arena in the 1960s to give broad-stroke guidance about what should happen in Mission Valley and other areas of San Diego. Too bad more people didn't listen. In later decades, he was the man to call for a reality check on the role of

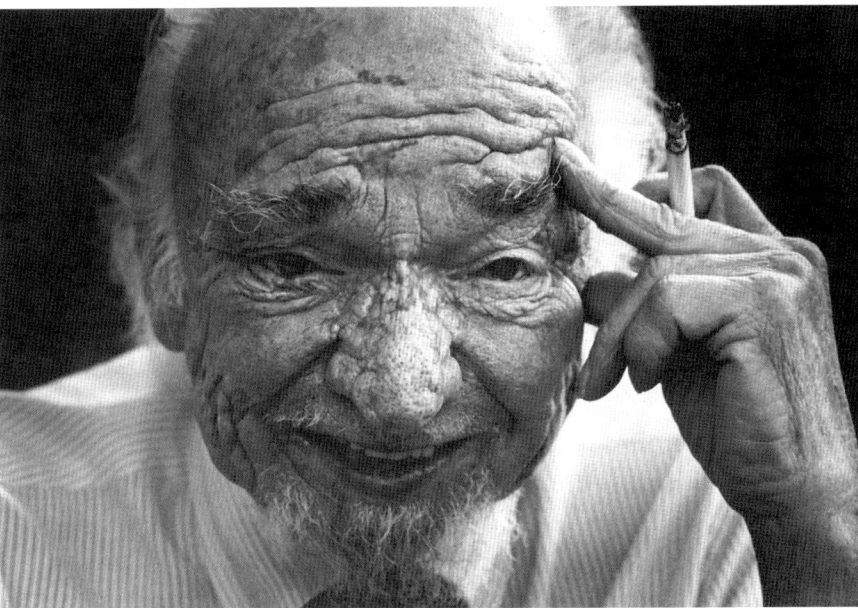

San Diego architect Sim Bruce Richards, 1908-1983, Hubbell's mentor and primary influence. *(Photo by Greg Voitjo)*

architects and artists in the city, and for answers to questions about design ethics.

Patience when appropriate, curiosity, flexibility, a designer's responsibility to the city, and the joy in the differences between one person and another. Those were some of the lessons from Architect Richards. He was a good teacher for Hubbell.

Most architectural writers have a difficult time trying to categorize someone like Hubbell. The easy solution is to place him in the group of designers belonging to what's loosely known as the organic school. The principles of Frank Lloyd Wright are at its core and its branches are architects such as Bruce Goff, Bart Prince, Herb Greene, Donald MacDonald and many other "Friends of Kebyar," an organization formed to extol the virtues of organic form. It's too easy to say that these are the guys who design buildings that look like chickens, mushrooms, or just slightly manipulated mounds of dirt.

But comparing one individualist to another, even if they receive the same newsletters and speak at the same conferences, is not a satisfactory solution. Sometimes it's best to ask the individual himself about how he got to be the way he is.

Although Hubbell agrees that Saarinen, Wright, and of course, Richards influenced him, he provides a clearer picture:

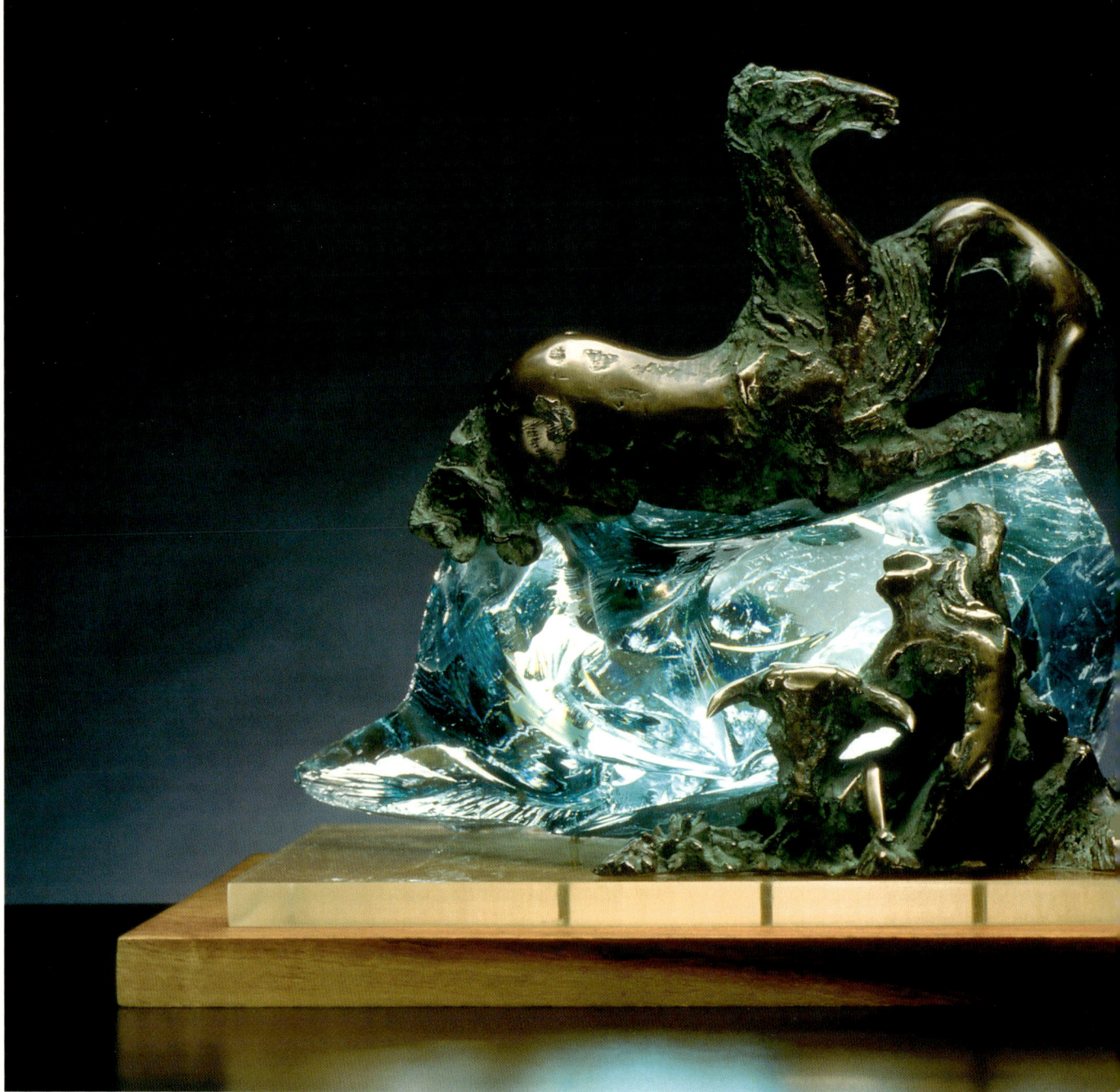

"As a kid, I had trouble in school and in understanding adults. I escaped into nature," he said recently. "It seems to me that there are two rivers in this human predicament we're in. One runs to nature and the other to the rational mind. Wright, Saarinen and Bruce bridged the two. They brought order, at least temporarily, to nature. That's where they dwelled, and where I do, too."

Nature was the core of Wright. The patterns of the lakes, granite outcroppings, trees, and the behaviors of animals and humans were close to Saarinen's spine, son of Finland that he was. Wright influenced Saarinen, and Saarinen influenced Wright, although Wright wouldn't admit it. Charles Rennie Mackintosh of Scotland influenced both of them. Wright drew from Japan and the Aztec culture. Richards's trips to Japan were among his favorites; he often talked of placing windows to frame views of nature that looked like Japanese nature paintings, with every tree, every branch, and the preferably foggy horizon line falling in exactly the right place in the composition.

Views from Hubbell windows are similar. "Wright and Saarinen learned from being exposed to other people's work and from their own experiences — nothing happens in a vacuum—but everything they did was absolutely their own," Hubbell said. "They made it theirs."

Hubbell has accomplished this, as well. His work is unmistakably his, whether he's working alone, with three helpers, with community groups to build parks or schools, or with American and Russian architecture students to build an amphitheater in Vladivostok.

"It is fundamental that whatever forms a man brings forth through honest work, those forms will not be entirely convincing unless they are a true expression of his life—his emotions, his thoughts, and his aspirations," Eliel Saarinen wrote to his students in 1948. "His art, at best, is a significant testimony of his integrity of mind and spirit, the product of his real personality. No work of art in any field can be considered a work of art unless it reveals the basic nature of the artist himself."

With Hubbell, his own nature is in every line, every stone.

And so is Nature.

Kaiser was the editor of Hidden Leaves, *the Ilan-Lael Foundation's quarterly publication in the mid-1980s. She was the architecture critic for the* San Diego Union-Tribune *from 1984-1993. She is the author of numerous books and articles on architectural subjects.*

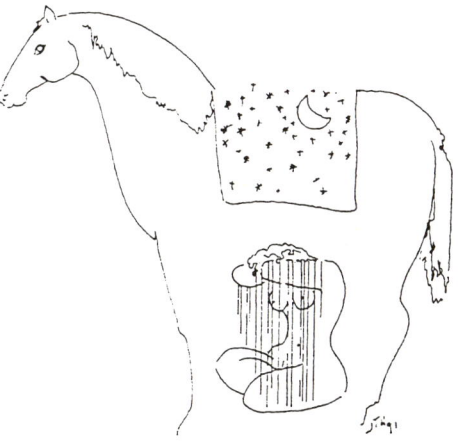

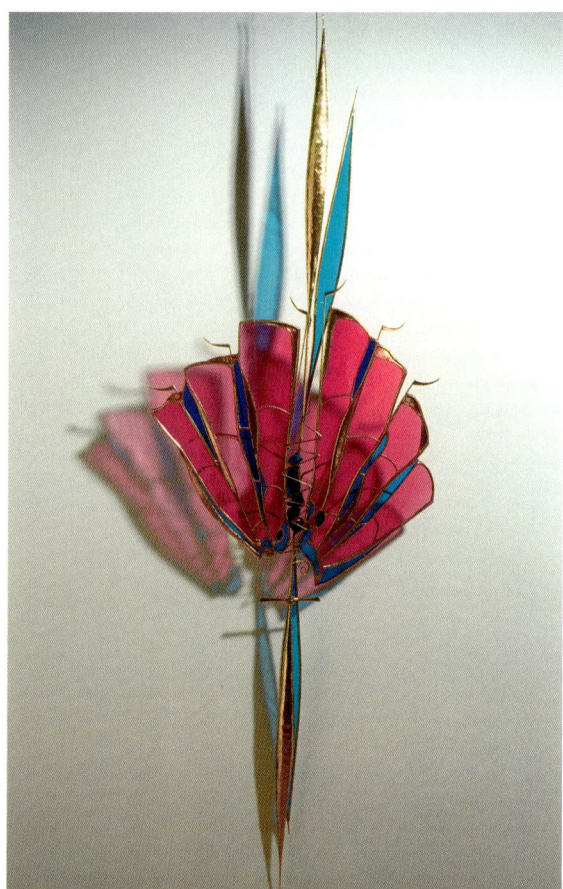

"Blue Meadow," cast bronze and glass, 13" x 14", 1986. *(Photo by Gene Faulkner)*

"Untitled," stained glass window with brass, 1990. Loaned by Dr. Josephine Von Herzen. *(Photo by Gene Faulkner)*

Four walls
 a prison makes
but if within
 a flower grows,
four walls
 a garden makes.

"The shape of a leaf serves, expresses the unique function of that particular leaf. Does the shape of a building or sound of a symphony serve and express the unique spiritual needs of the composer and his age (time)?"

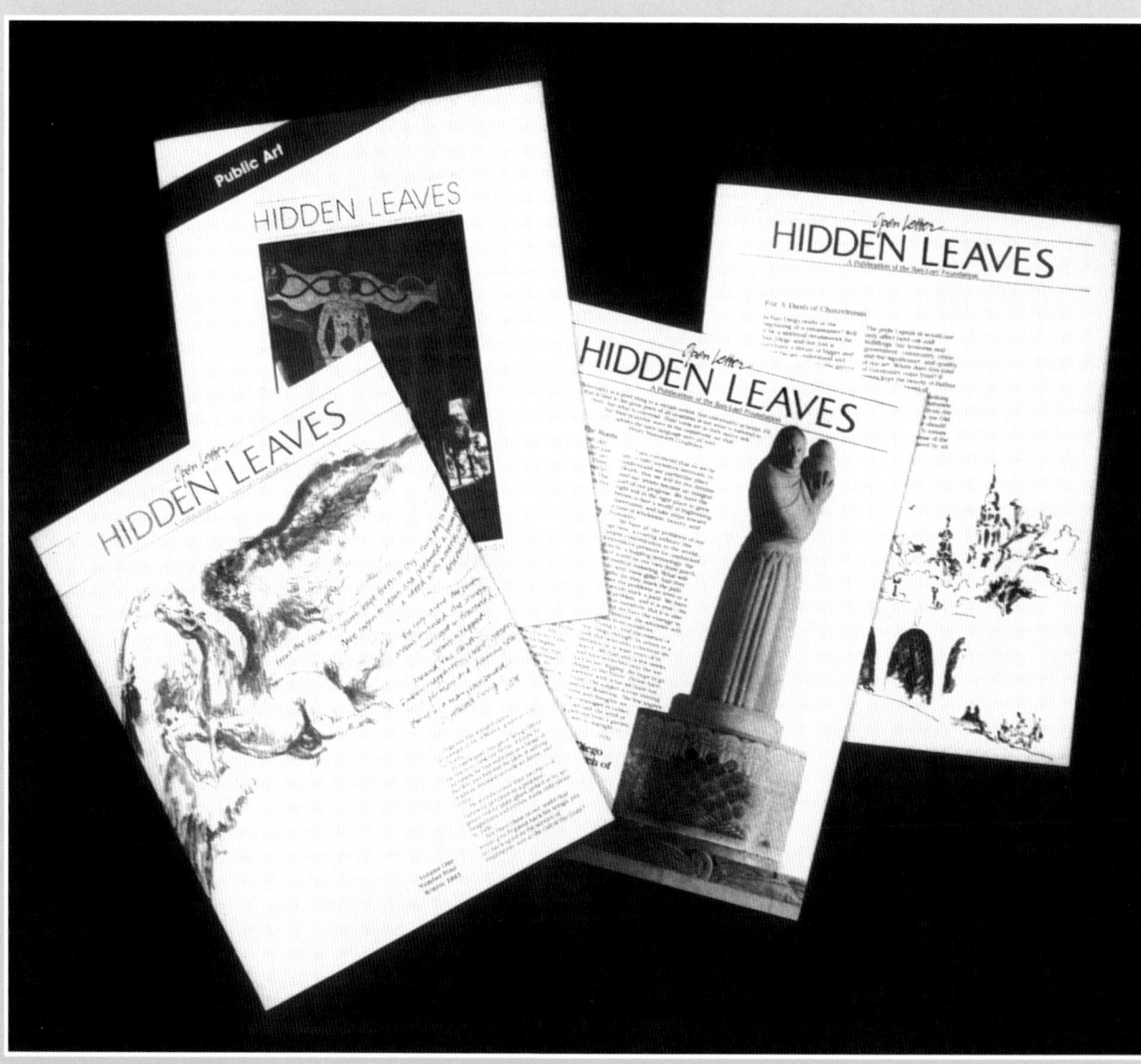

The first four issues of *Hidden Leaves* magazine, co-edited by
Kay Kaiser and James Hubbell, 1982-1987.

THE ILAN LAEL FOUNDATION

In 1982, James Hubbell and friends founded the Ilan Lael Foundation, a non-profit educational foundation with the aim of helping artists become more involved within the fabric of the San Diego region.

    Its first efforts to start a school were unsuccessful, but as membership grew—eventually close to 1,400 members—its involvement in the city grew as well. Backed by the Foundation, five issues of *Hidden Leaves* were published, with Kay Kaiser and later Clare White as editors, exploring the visual arts, the mysteries of the city, and the philosophies of change. Over a ten year period, the Foundation hosted and co-hosted over 55 events—lectures, seminars, videos, and furniture shows. Each year for six years, co-sponsored by the Tijuana Cultural Center, a juried bi-city sculpture exhibition was held.

    By 1992 the first phase of Ilan Lael had slowed, and its involvement in"Soil and Soul"—a design/build, hands-on student workshop—took the forefront. By this time Hubbell's involvement with the design of Tijuana"s Collegio de Esperanza and Vladivostok's "Soul and Earth Friendship Sister City Park," was taking the major part of his time.

    Ilan Lael's initial desire to build a school seemed finally to be happening, though in a different way. Since the formation of the Pacific Rim Foundation in 1995—also a Hubbell-inspired group—a search has begun for a San Diego park location suitable to symbolize global unity and encourage cultural interchange between the family of Pacific Rim cities.

    Hubbell's invitation to mount a retrospective show of his work at Moscow's Shusev Central Museum of Architecture in October 1998, marks another phase of his busy career, exploring art as a means of diplomacy and love of nature as a tool for change, keeping an eye on where the world is headed in the new century.

From each hill and rock
    I hear a song
Life adrift within.

    All parts are mine
    Earth and river
    Field and tree
Interlaced with man.

    Song of wind wrapped in sea
      of rain and stars
Sprinkled in the sand.

Mud and life and I
    Together
Quiet worship bring.

"It is my belief that philosophy is a verb."

Kuchumaa Chapel, Rancho La Puerta, Tecate, Mexico, 1990. An outdoor chapel and rest space built by Hubbell, Milenko Matanovic, and the Soil & Soul apprentice program as a tribute to Kuchumaa, a sacred mountain on the U.S./Mexico border. Built in 11 days by 13 students; sponsored by Rancho La Puerta. *(Photo by John Durant)*

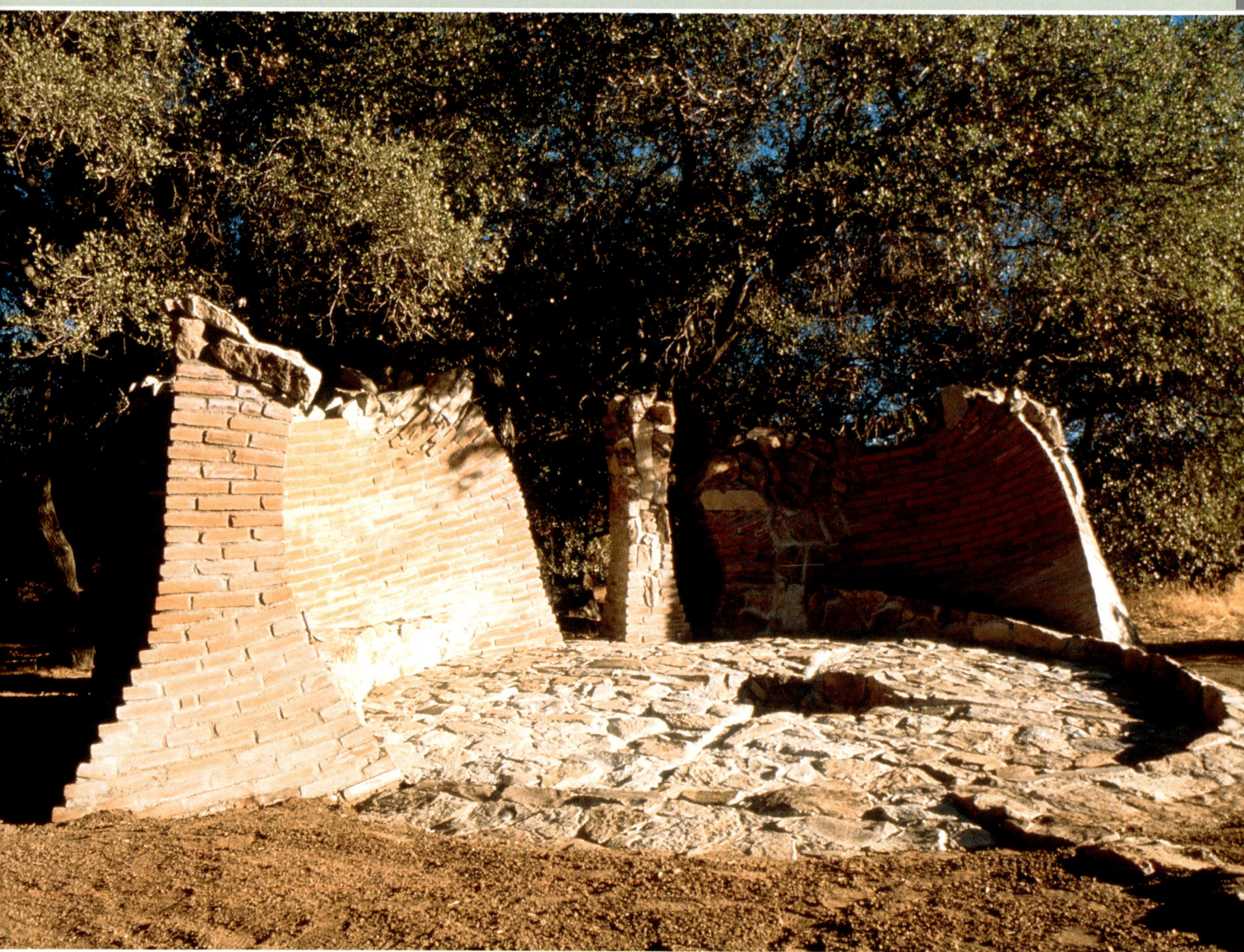

In a Soil & Soul workshop each person contributes something uniquely necessary to the aesthetic whole. The participants respect the earth, their materials, and each other's creativity. They deal with political tensions, climatic or bureaucratic disasters, and personality problems. Sometimes they suffer. But they keep on working, for the exuberance of James Hubbell's aesthetic is energizing. The exuberance of beauty is the antidote to violence, fear, and addiction . . . The beauty that is truth that is beauty isn't empirical; it's organic. It's as necessary as air.　　　　　　　　—Suzanne Sklar

Collegio de Esperanza, pre-school and primary school being built in Colonia Esperanza, a Tijuana suburb. Sponsored by the Americas Foundation. Designed by Hubbell, erected with the help of volunteers. 1990 - present.

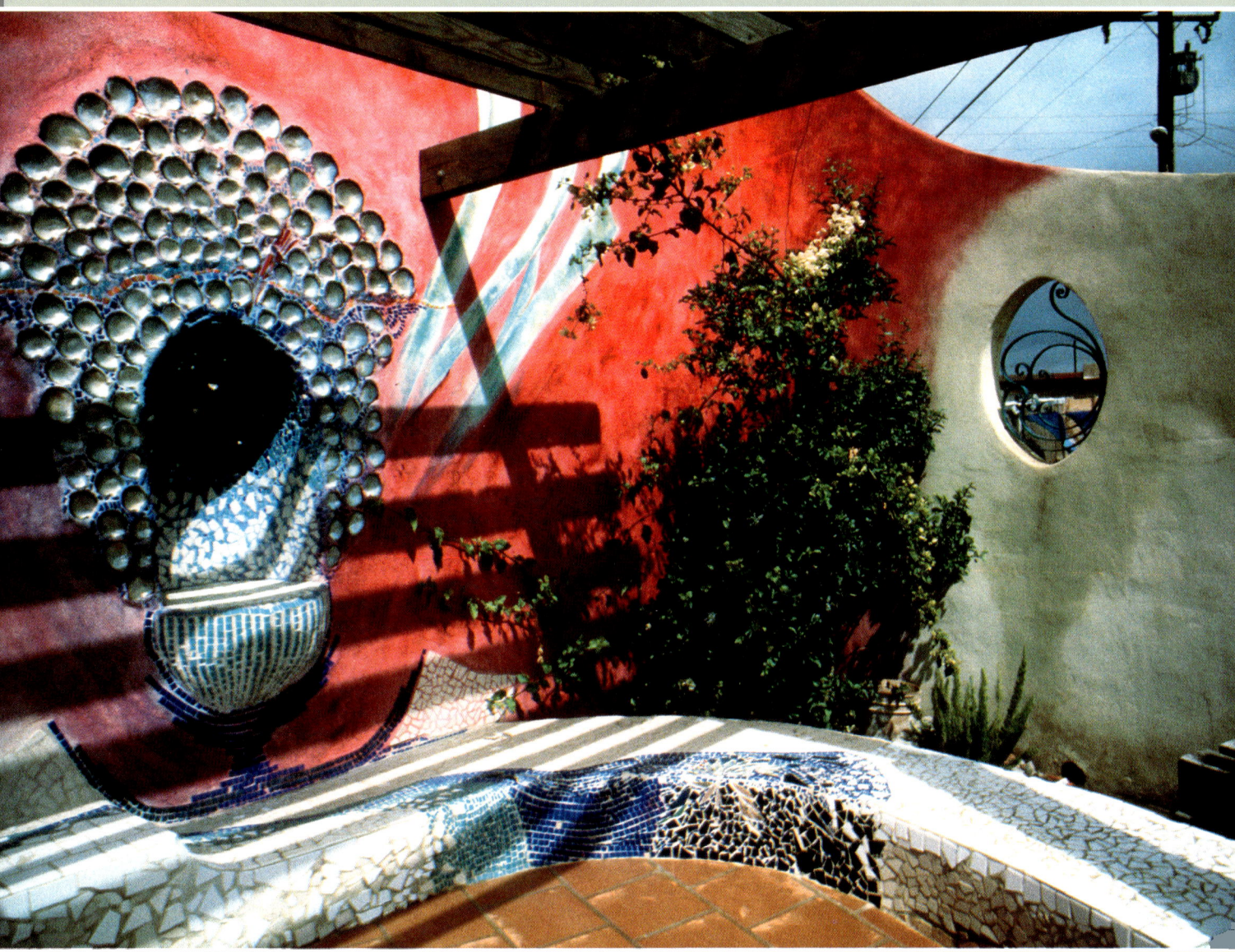

Each day   As a flower
     The air is like nectar
Even the sad,   Part of the song.
     To work is to dance
     To live is to worship
     To breathe is to Love . . .

"*Modern art depicts so carefully the modern predicament: line is the line of the subway, color is the color of plastic and neon, form is the form of the machine and all its parts. I believe I would prefer an art that comes from the earth and the sunset.*"

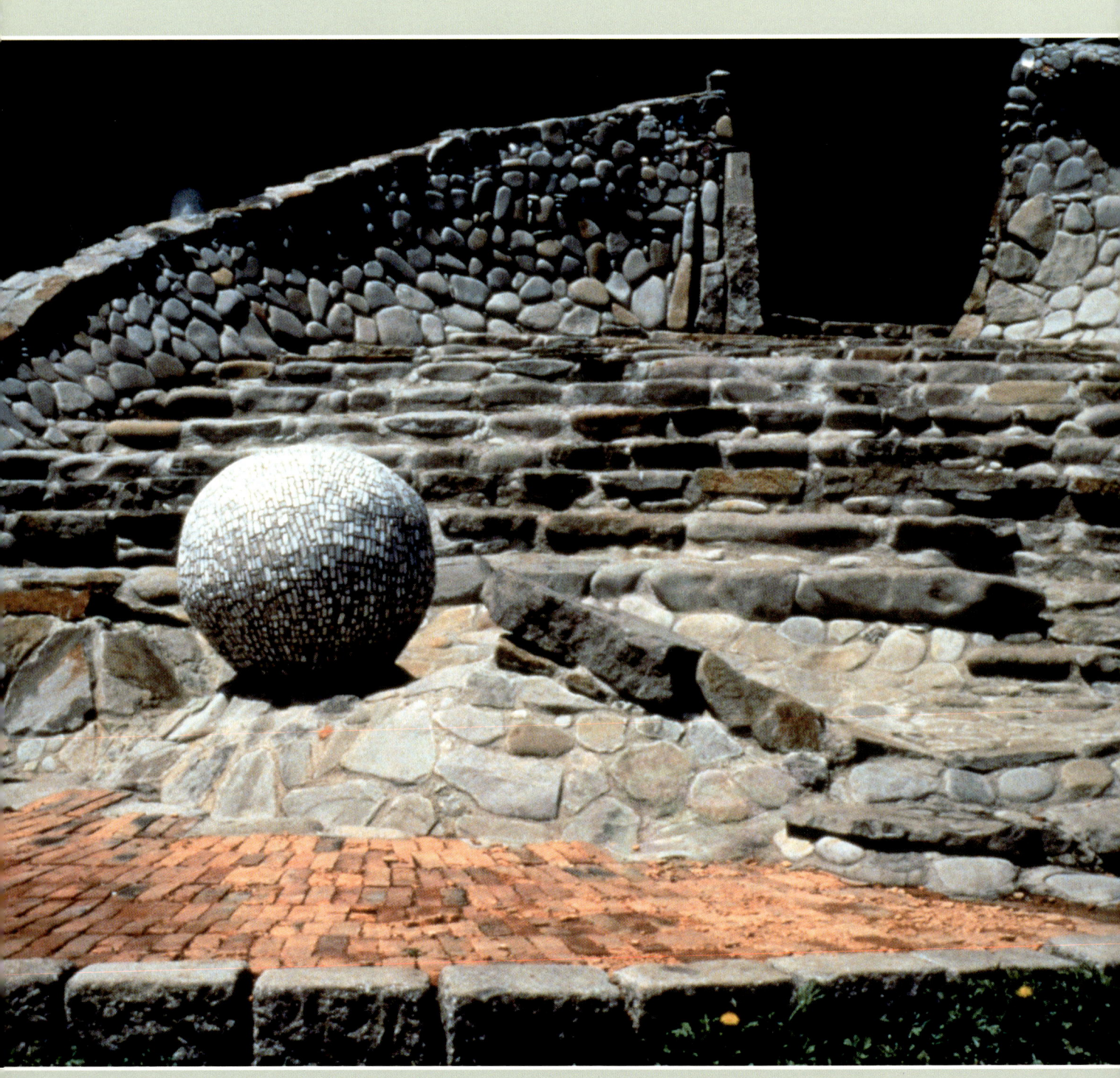

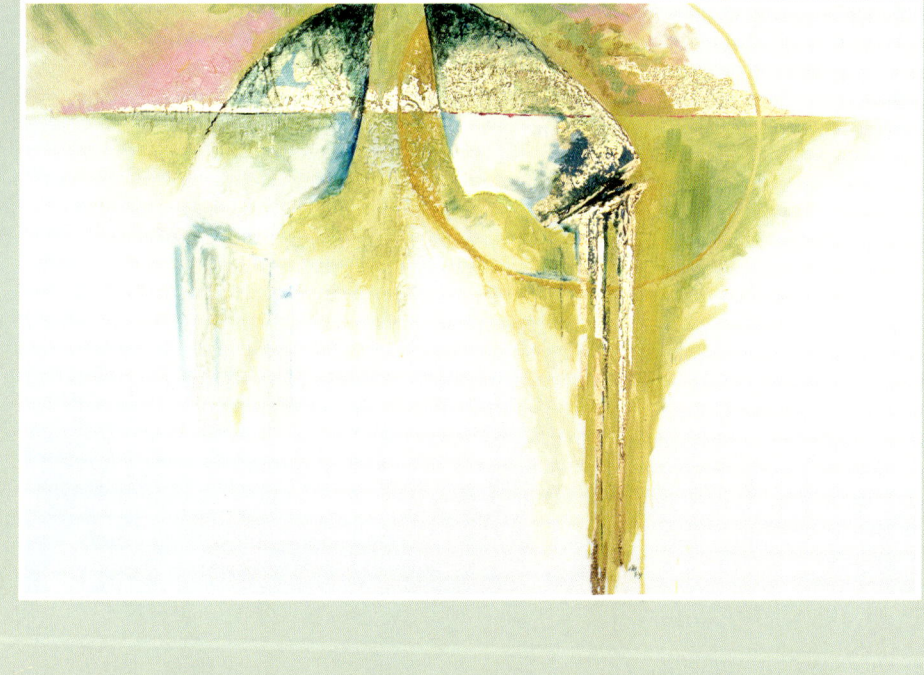

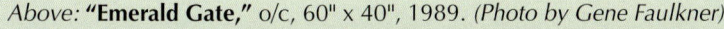

Above: **"Emerald Gate,"** o/c, 60" x 40", 1989. *(Photo by Gene Faulkner)*

Left: **"Soul and Earth Friendship and Sister City Park"** — Far Eastern State Technical University, Vladivostok, Russia, 1994, 1995. A design-and-build workshop completed in 21 days under the direction of Hubbell and Milenko Matanovic. Also involved were eight students from the U.S., one from Mexico, and twelve from Russia. Sponsored by the Technical University, City of Vladivostok, San Diego/Vladivostok Sister City Association, and the Ilan Lael Foundation.

Two columns stand
> waiting in a dark sea,
> crystal rocks
> spanned by light.
>> Far away
>> the call of an eagle.

When time brings
> the circle round,
> when chaos dims,
> the last dance past,
> only then
>> to walk the Emerald Gate.

The essence of the Soil & Soul method is that it compresses what might otherwise be a long and convoluted process into a very intense and continuous movement during which the group first envisions and conceptualizes the artwork, and then, through the guidance of the lead artists who serve as the synthesizers, designs the artwork. Then, without pause, the group begins the construction of the artwork.
> — *Milenko Matanovic*

"How can it be that an artist can know how a small piece of a large work will eventually relate to the entire work when he doesn't know what the entire work will be like, or even how the small piece relates to the world he is not even conscious of? The only word that comes to mind is "faith."

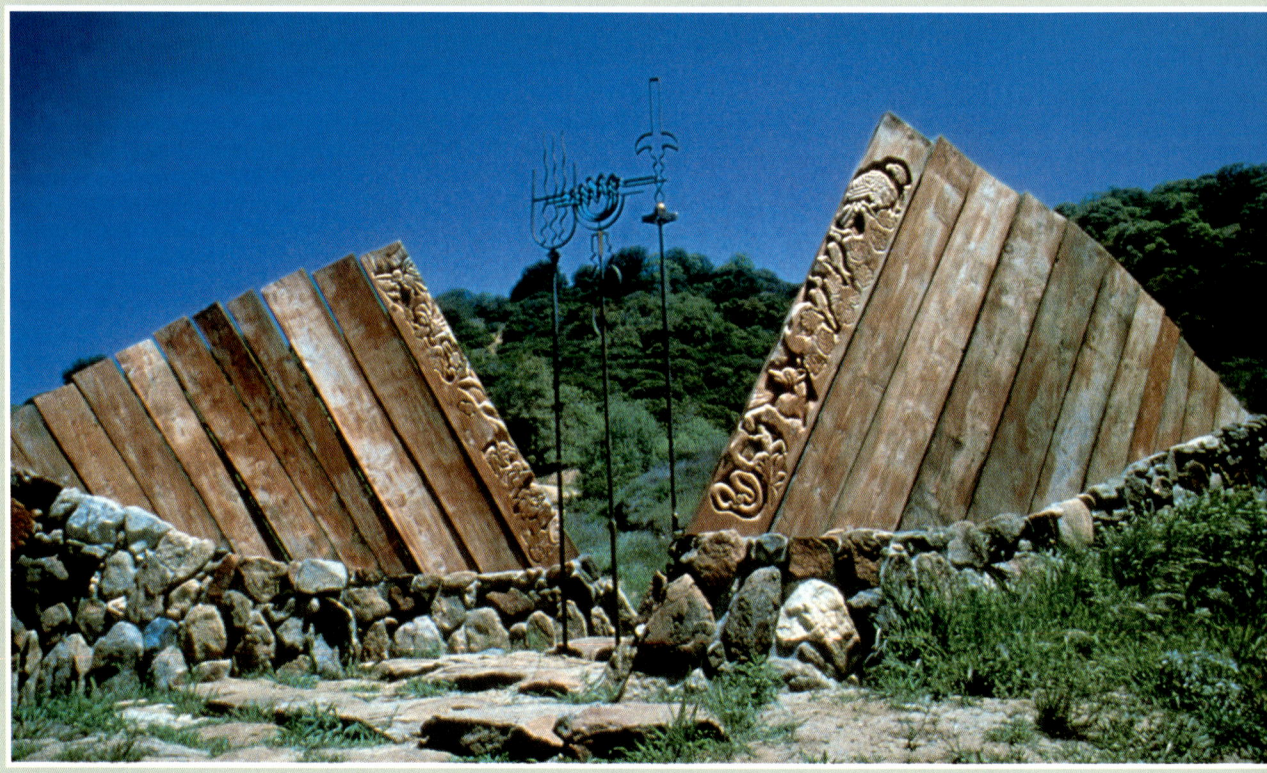

Volcan Mountain Preserve, entrance gate and sculpture, Julian, California. A volunteer construction project organized by Vicky Bergstrom, designed and supervised by Hubbell, 1993.

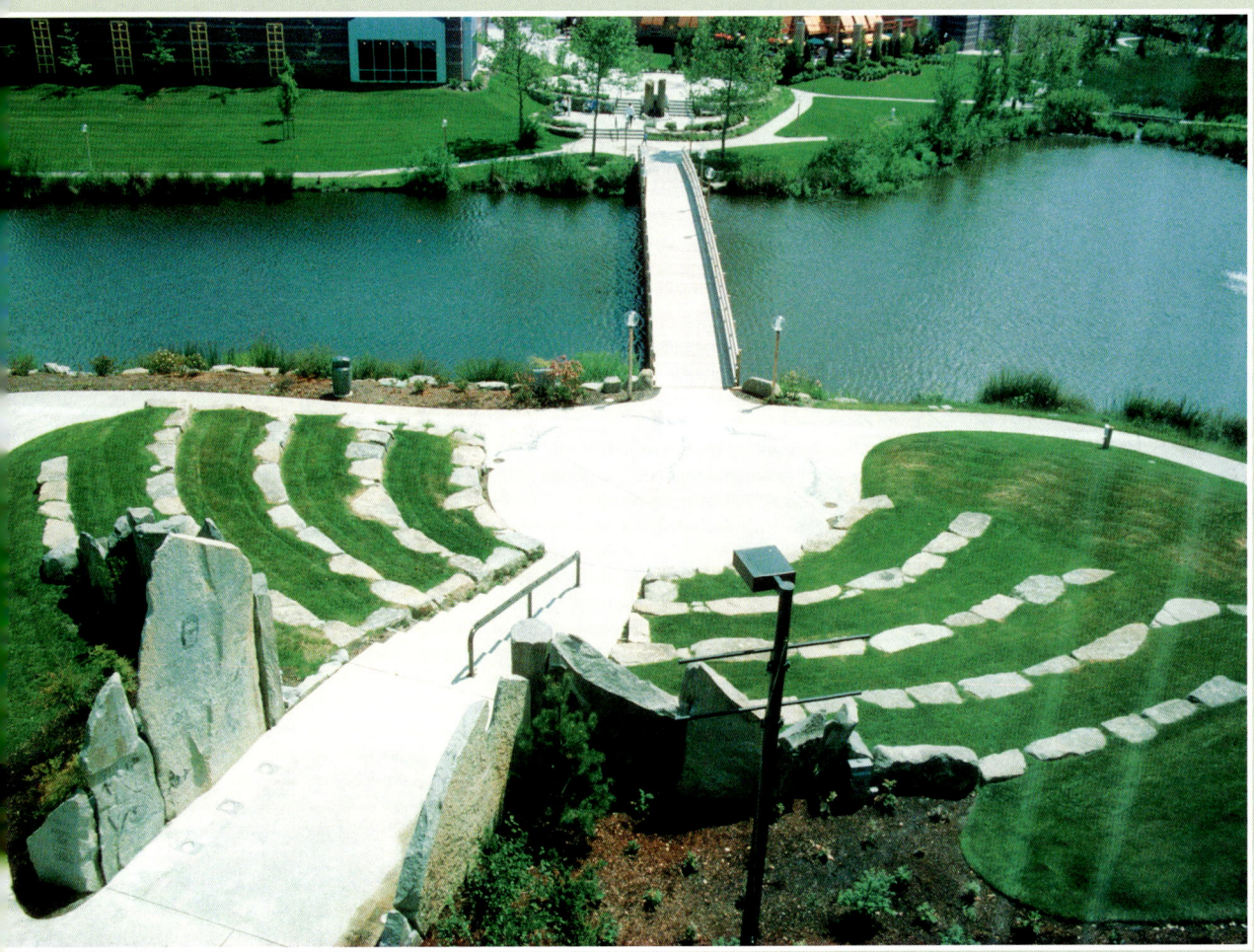

Pickering Historical Park, Issaquah, Washington. A memorial to the first governor of Washington state and his family. Consists of an amphitheater and large plaza which serves as an extensive shopping area for the town of Issaquah. 1993, 1994. *(Photo by Milenko Matanovic)*

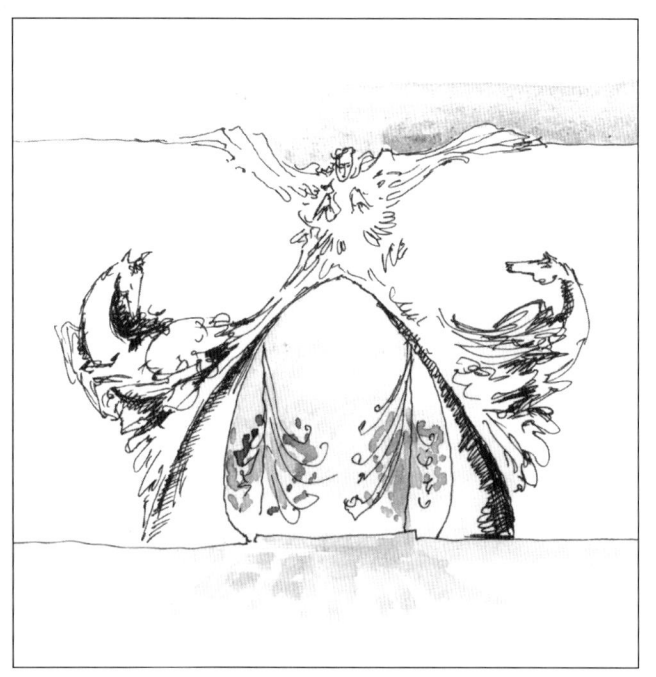

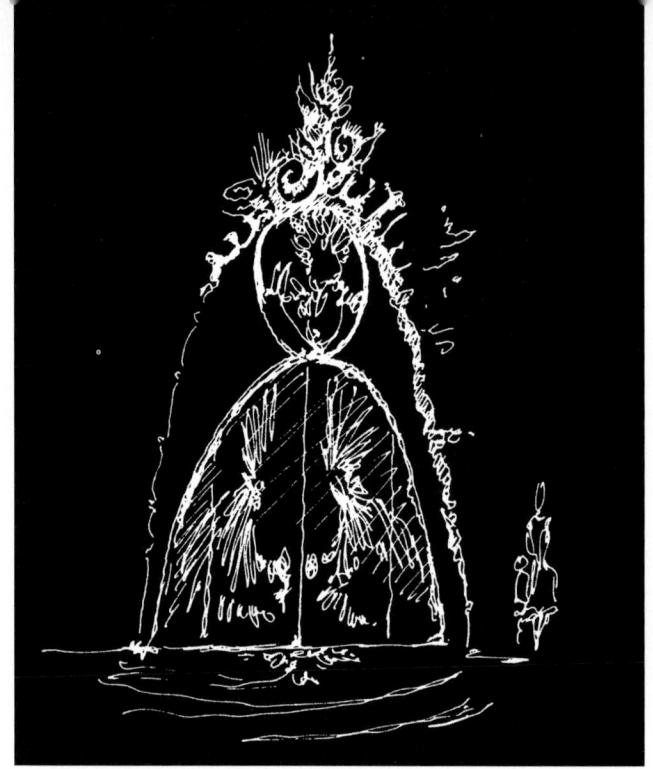

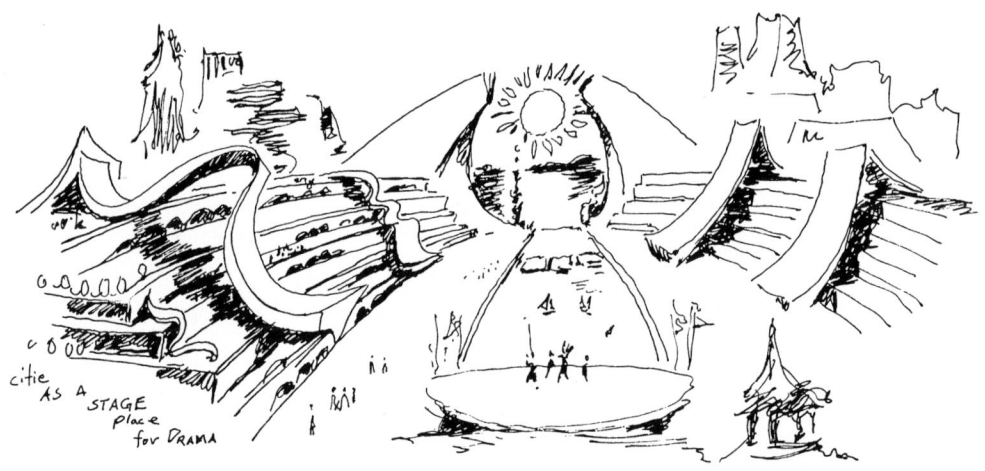

citie AS A STAGE place for DRAMA

Selected idea sketches from a series of notebooks done over the past 35 years.

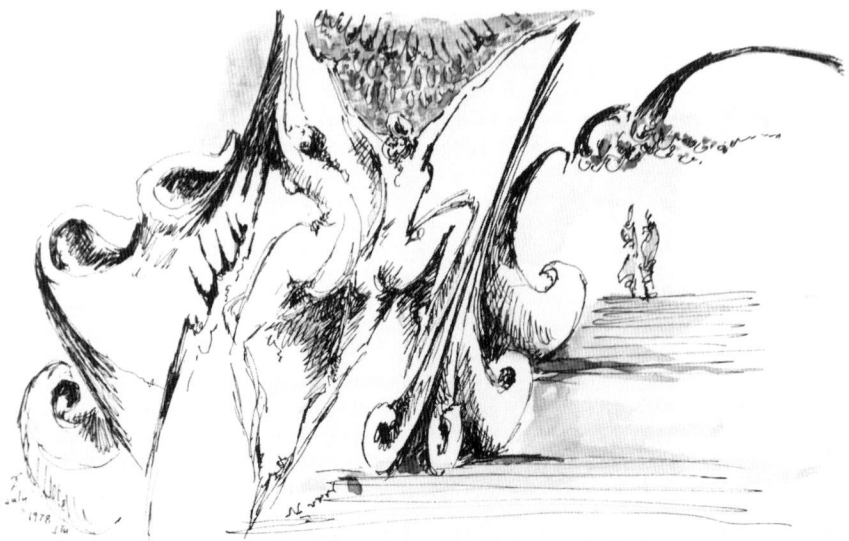

I tell you, you are a seed.
    You are the earth,
        A warm stone.

You are a drop of rain,
    Or like the immortal foam,
        Breath of the sea.

There is no end to the stars
    And your eyes
No wing that will not guide you
    No love, you are not of
        And none that is not for you.

    You are as the earth
    My love and my lover.

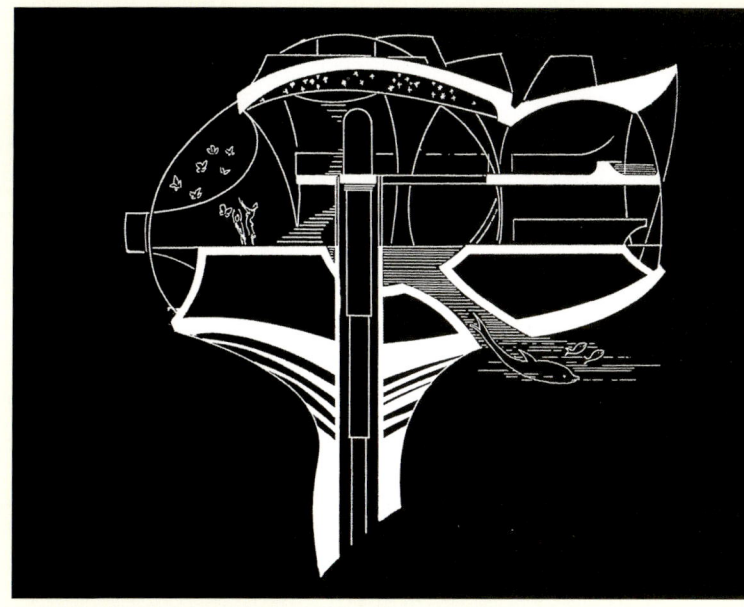

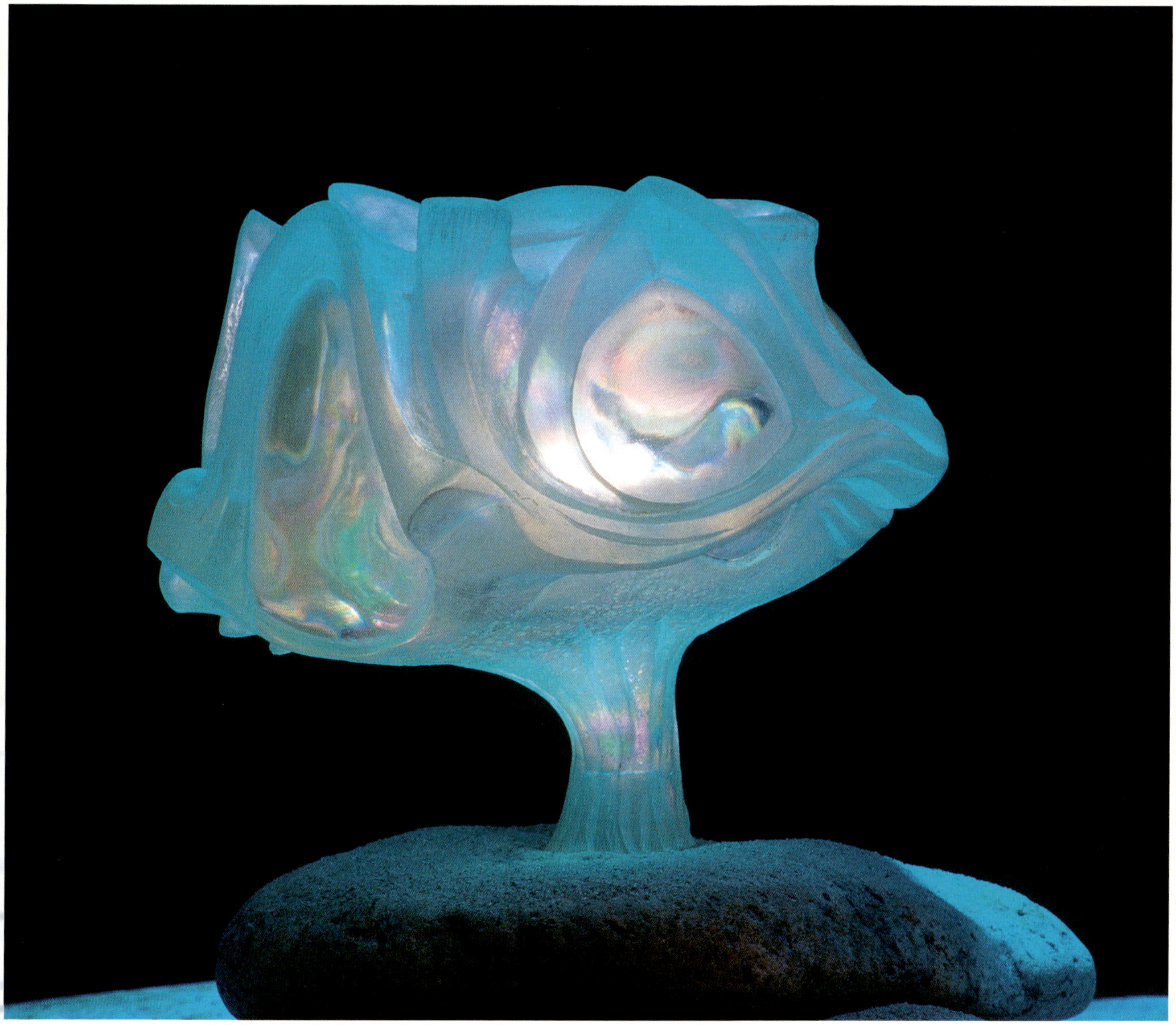

"Deep Dream," an underwater house. The site for this house is 300 feet off the coast of La Jolla, 60' below sea level. Designed for Elizabeth Marshall in 1995, by James and Drew Hubbell, but not yet built. *(Photo by Chuck Kimball)*

"Approaching Storm," watercolor, 7" x 10", 1994.

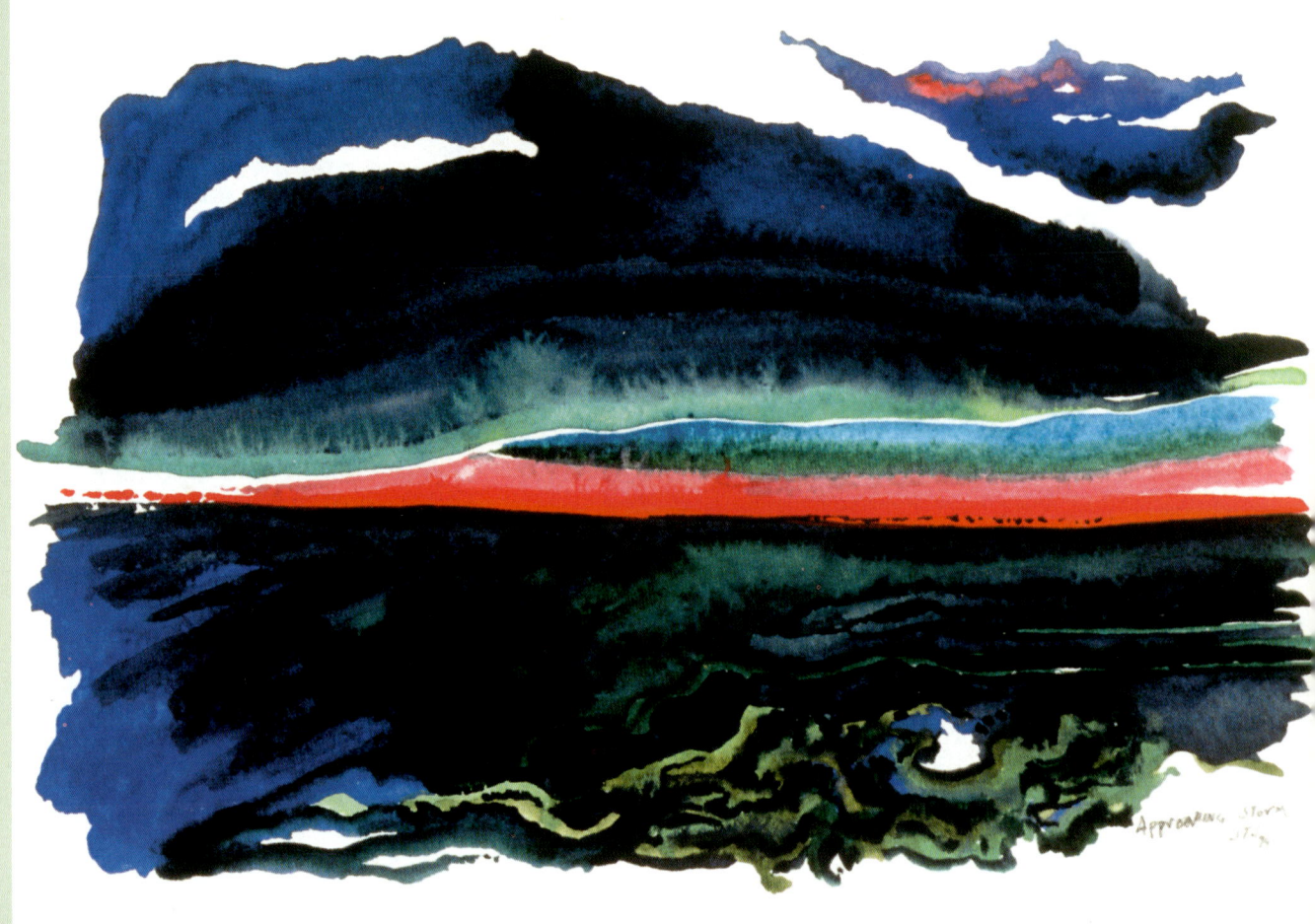

Wild things
    Run wild.
        Bring wind.
            Sweep the heart.

                Wild things
                    Sweet change
                        Belonging to dreams
                            In hidden places.

"Though we desire beauty, we wish for truth. Yet to name them, to lay them bare upon the page, is to render truth and beauty lifeless, useless. The path is more to set their glow on the horizon of one's mind, then every day to take the hundred small steps toward their glow. The path is one of effort and faith. To journey toward truth and beauty is to embrace all life. Yet to believe one knows the heart of God is to render him immobile, to make his power, his joy lifeless."

Untitled, watercolor and metallic paint, 1996.

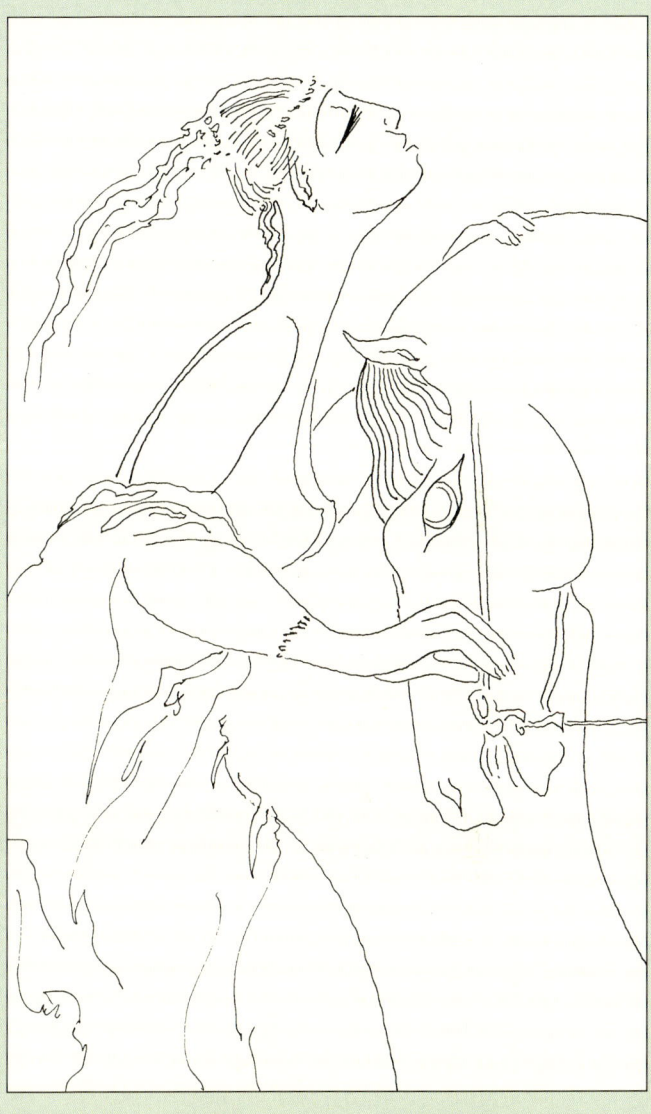

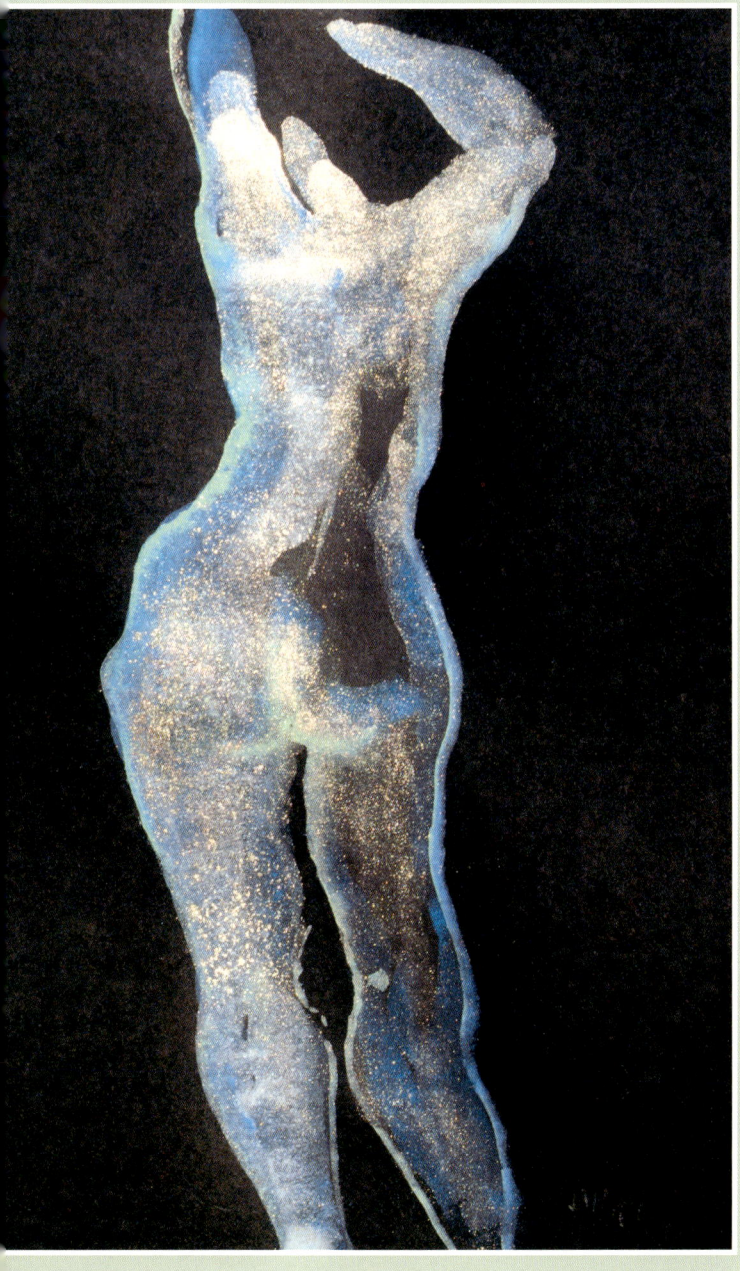

"An artist's task is the transformation of concept-to-reality into an emotional, workable reality, a contemporary relevance now."

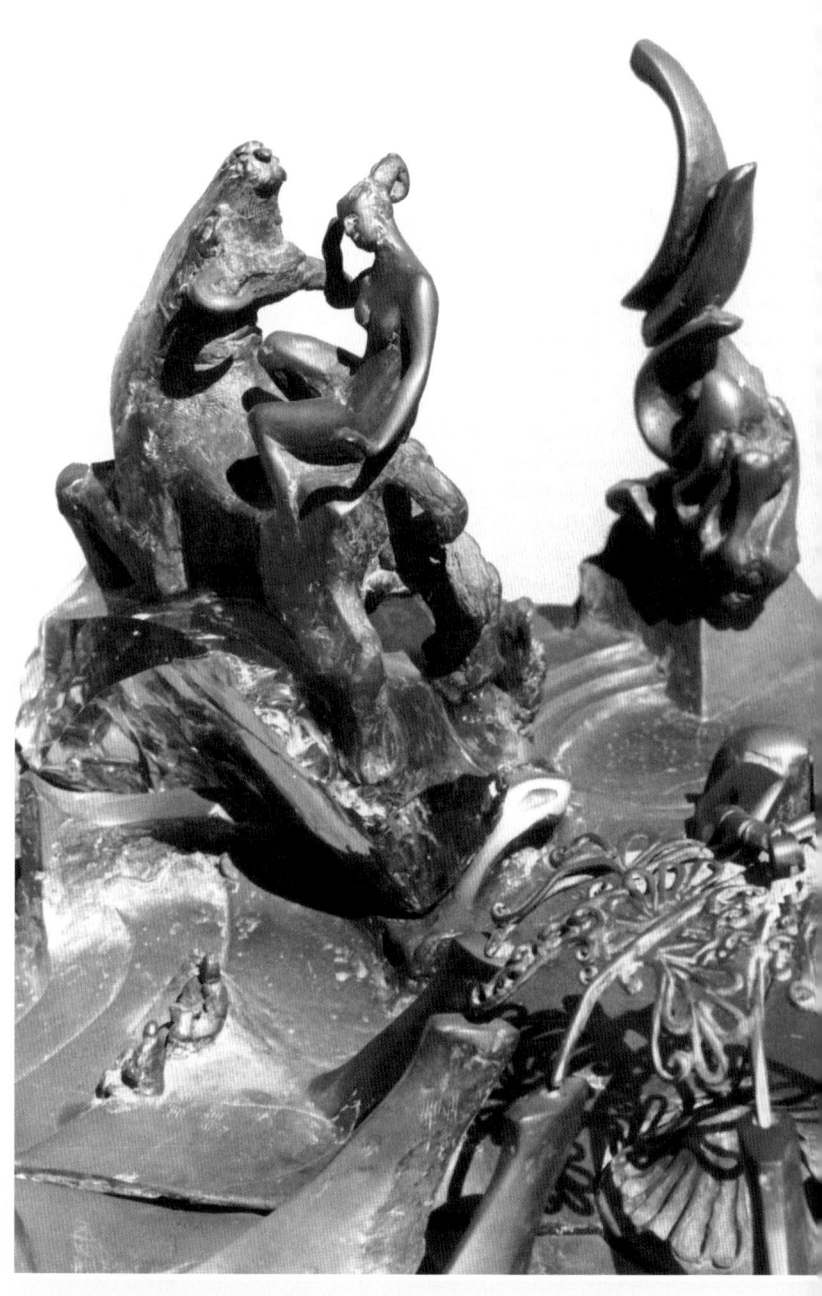

Imaginary park (detail), bronze casting, 26" x 30" x 12", 1979

"Try to imagine a forest where the cycle of life and death were broken, where there was no death. You would have to remove time and growth. Life and death exist wholly dependent on each other."

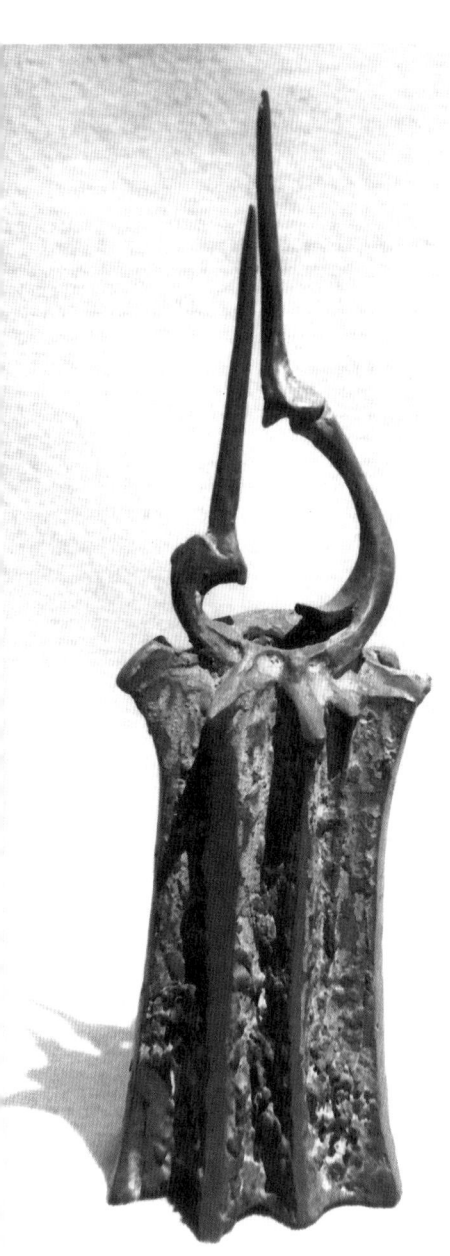

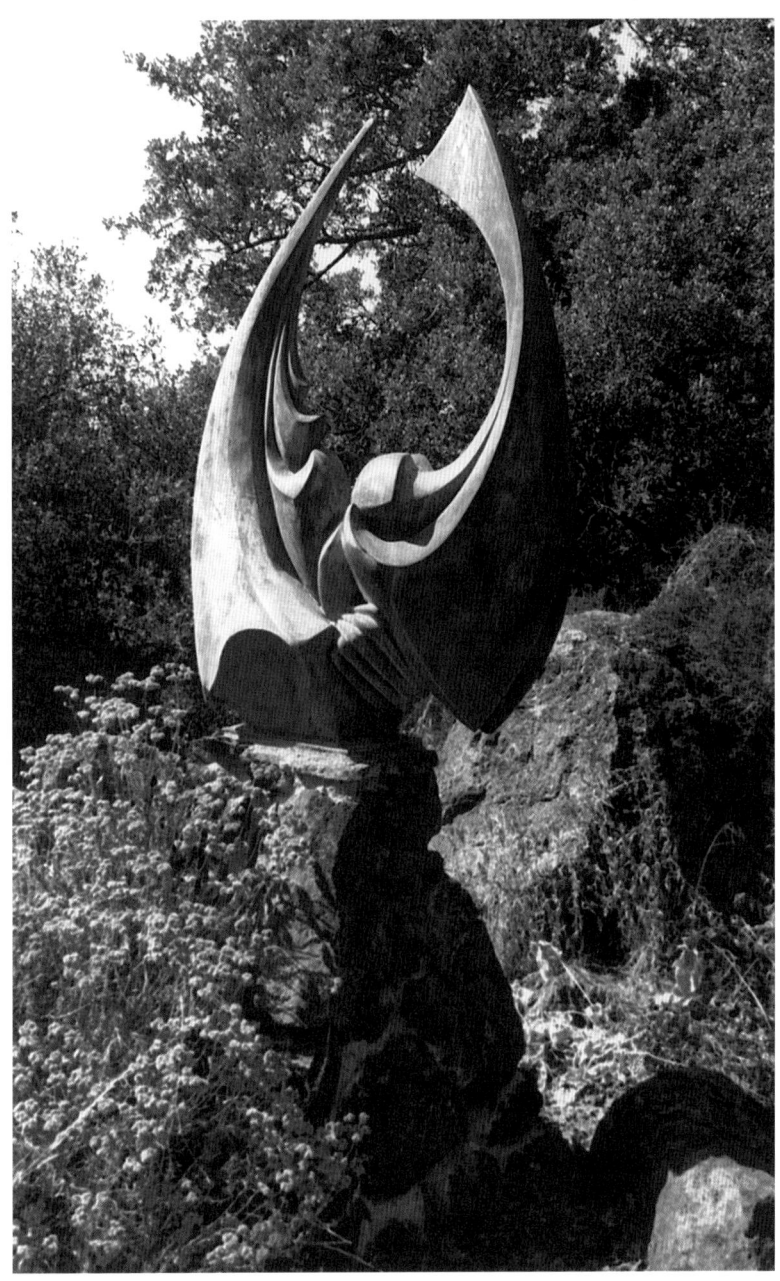

Bronze vase, 12" x 4", 1968.

Bronze sculpture. Original commissioned by Boyd and Marilyn Deel. This copy of the original in collection of the artist. *(Photos by Robert Perine)*

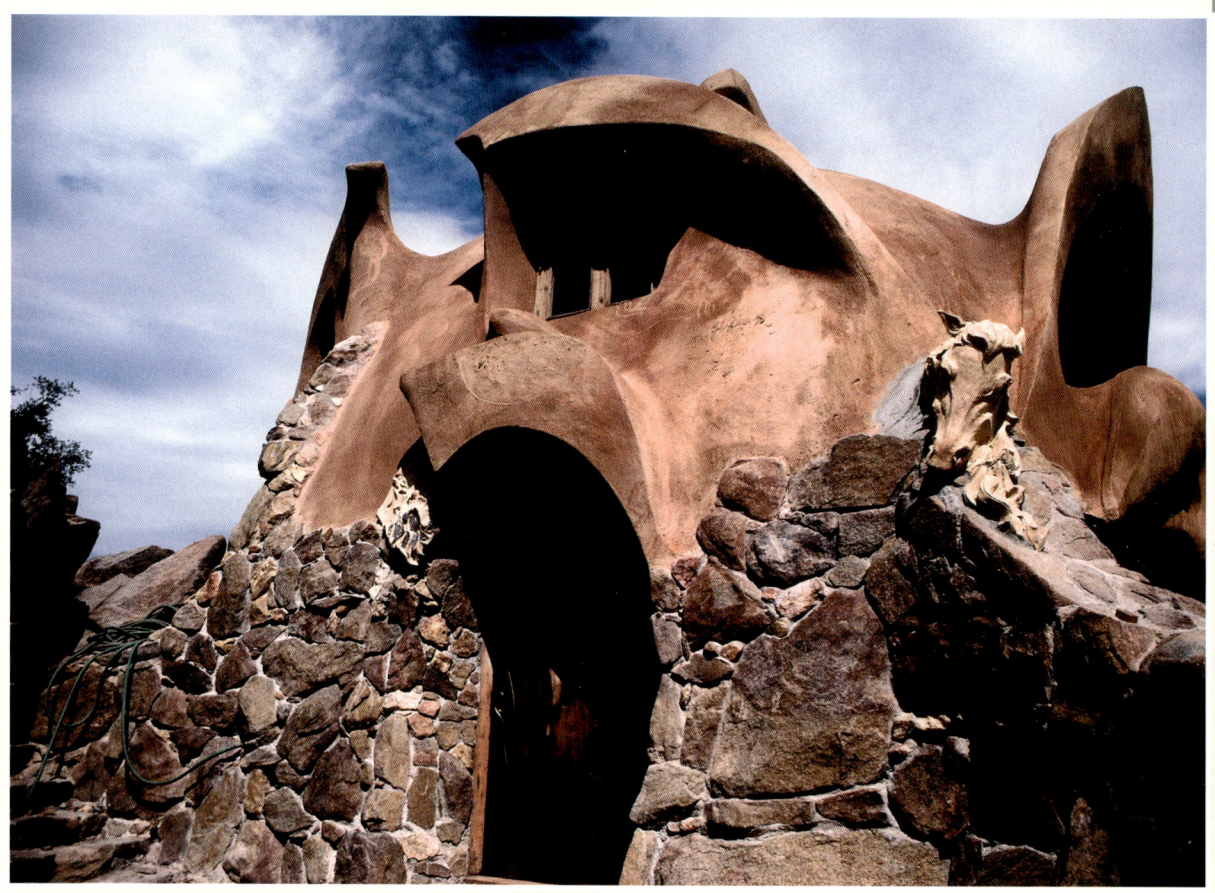

Rainbow Hill, home of Phil and Wendy Gay in Julian California, 1991.

Davis Art Center design, Davis
California, floor plan and north
elevation, 1979. (Never built)

*"To give of love
or beauty is not
always rewarding
in material ways.
After all, birds do
not get paid to sing."*

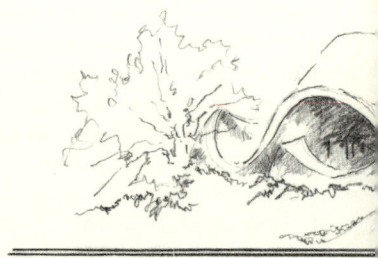

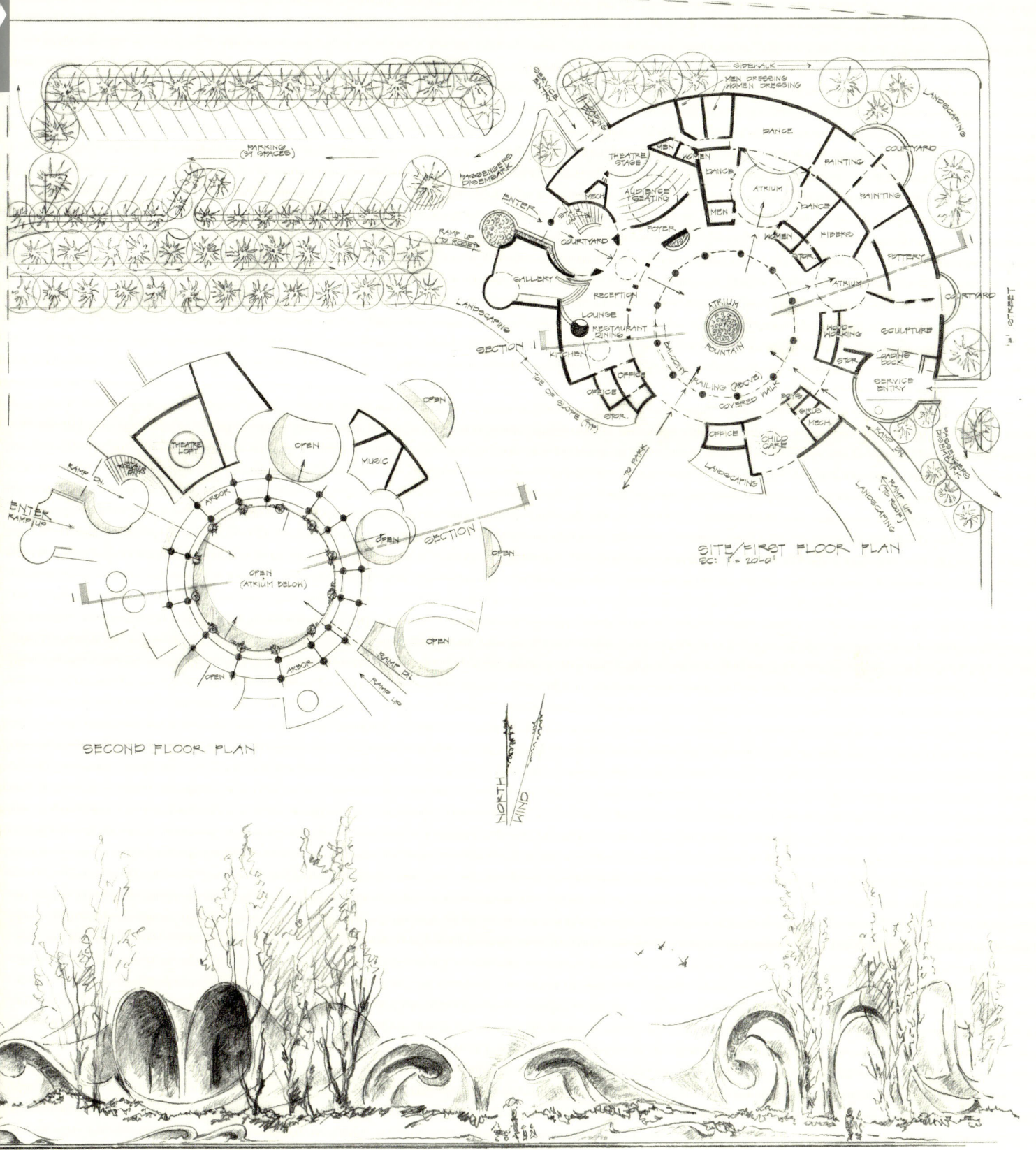

COVELL BOULEVARD

SIDEWALK

MEN DRESSING
WOMEN DRESSING

LANDSCAPING

DANCE

PAINTING

COURTYARD

THEATRE STAGE

MEN

WOMEN

DANCE

PAINTING

MECH

DANCE

ATRIUM

AUDIENCE SEATING

DANCE

FIBERS

MEN

POTTERY

COURTYARD

ENTER

FOYER

WOMEN

ATRIUM

GALLERY

STOR

ATRIUM

RECEPTION

ATRIUM FOUNTAIN

WOOD WORKING

SCULPTURE

LOUNGE

RESTAURANT DINING

BALCONY RAILING (ABOVE)

LOADING DOCK

KITCHEN

COVERED WALK

SERVICE ENTRY

OFFICE

OFFICE

BOYS

GIRLS

MECH

STOR

OFFICE

CHILD CARE

LANDSCAPING

SITE/FIRST FLOOR PLAN
SC: 1" = 20'-0"

RAMP UP (TO ROOF)

SERVICE ENTRY

PASSENGER DISEMBARK

RAMP UP (TO ROOF)

PARKING (54 SPACES)

LANDSCAPING

SECTION

TOE OF SLOPE (TYP)

TO PARK

LANDSCAPING

RAMP UP (TO ROOF)

PASSENGER DISEMBARK

STREET

OPEN

THEATRE LOFT

OPEN

MUSIC

ENTER RAMP UP

ARBOR

OPEN

SECTION

OPEN (ATRIUM BELOW)

OPEN

RAMP DN

ARBOR

RAMP UP

OPEN

SECOND FLOOR PLAN

NORTH

WIND

NORTH ELEVATION

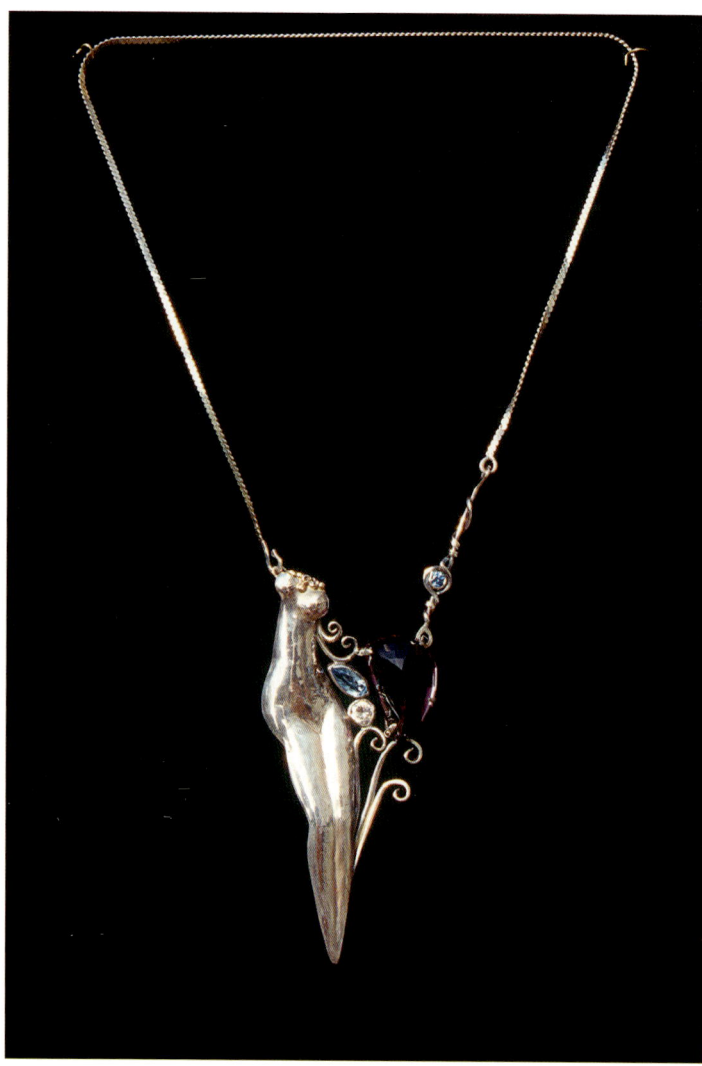

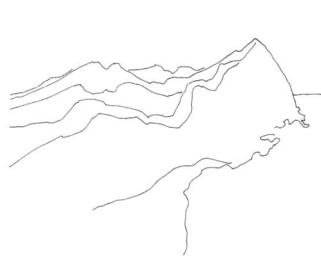

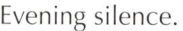

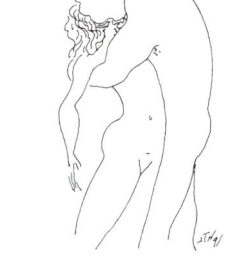

Evening silence.
    Quiet seas that lay a path
        To the sun.
Before, a dark violet Pacific
    framed by rows of
      orange-tipped surf
      nucleus given.

A quiet end
    at the edge of a continent
    at the edge of a day
      to sit and share the
      worries of the world
      small and fleeting.

The great Pacific,
    chapeled in the evening's
    universe,
      Moves in splendor
      dressed in rows of pearls,
      finds her rest.

"Lady With Amethyst," necklace of silver, gold, blue topaz, cz, blue cz, amethyst, 4½" x 2½", 1996.

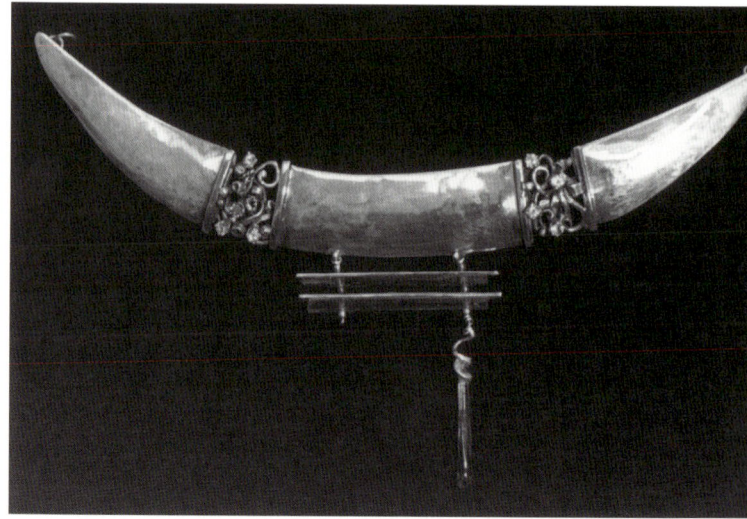

Raised Silver Necklace with 14K gold, citrine, and glass. 7" x 3", 1994.

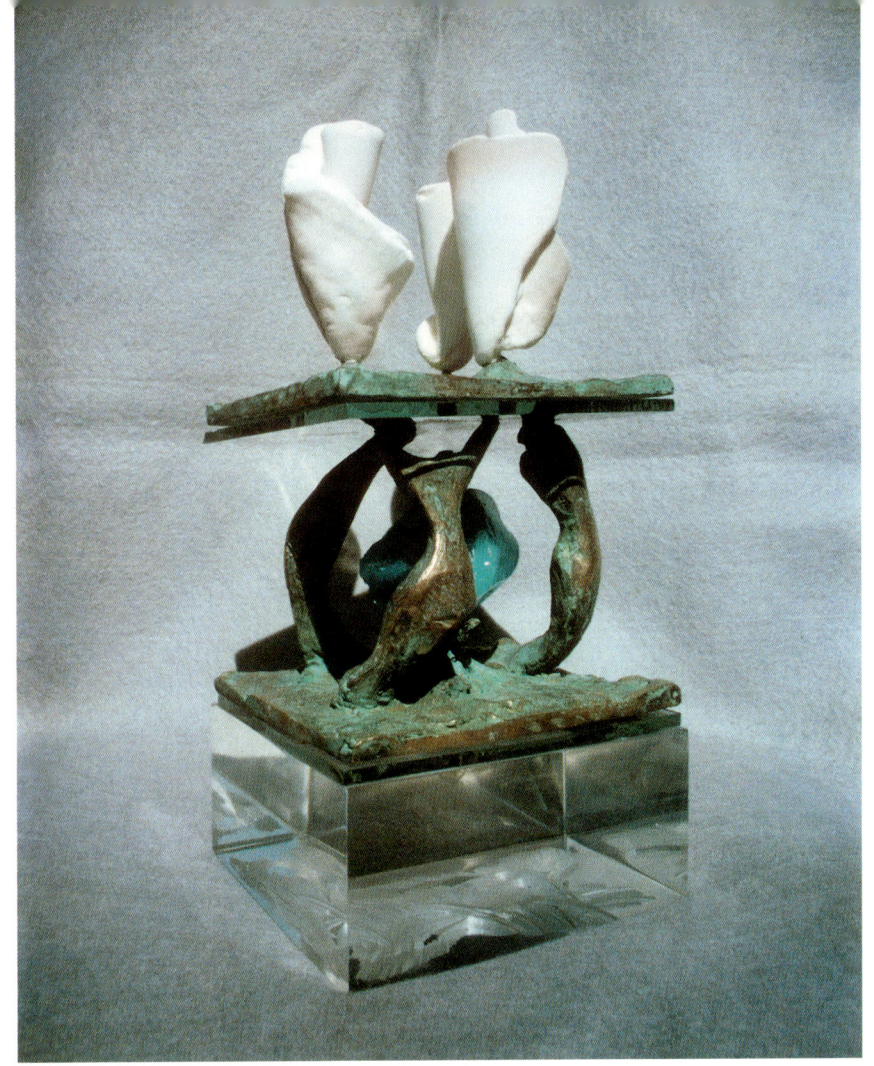

Above: **"Sea Shrine,"** cast bronze, glass, Plexiglas, and shells, 5½" sq. x 12" high. 1997.
(Photo by Cher Brown)

Glass sculpture, laminated glass,
forged silver, 11" x 17", 1986.
(Photo by Gene Faulkner)

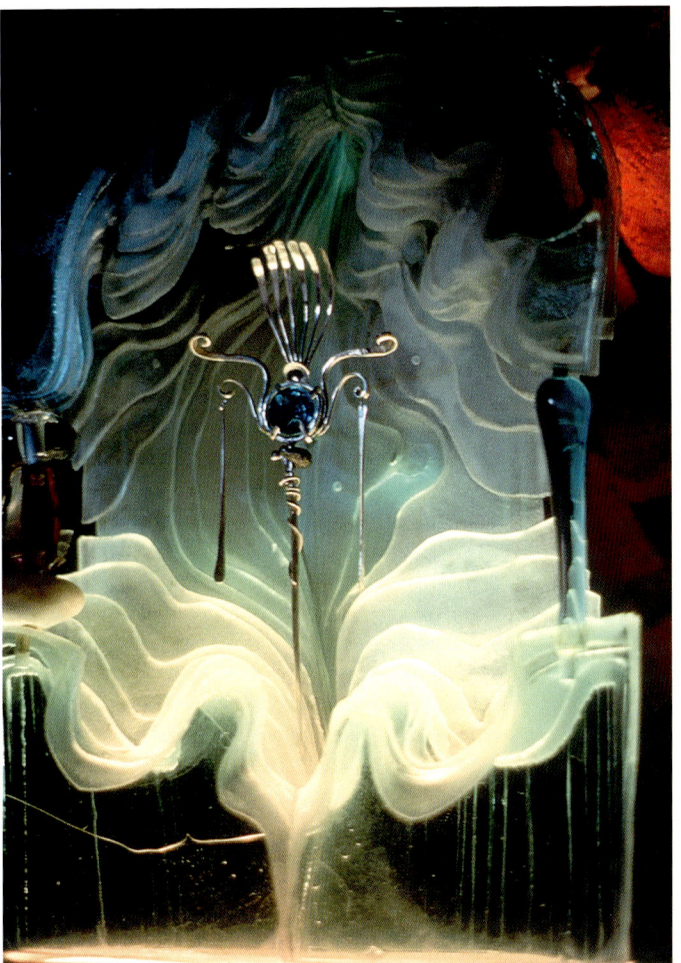

HUBBELL TIME LINE
(Partial List)

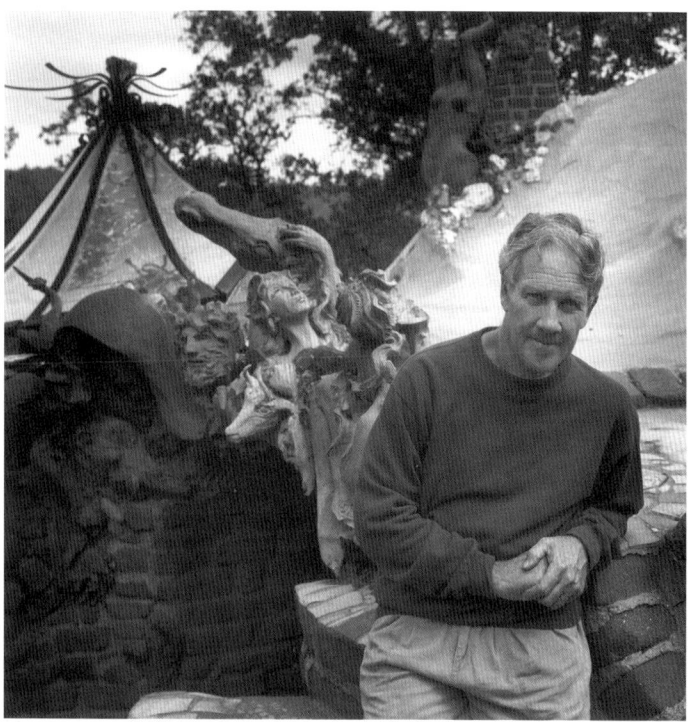

Photo by Don Musial

"I cannot change my shape, my face. I have been born to them. They are just there. But with my hands and my mind, with brick and clay, I may fashion my self."

1931 Born October 23. Lived in Connecticut, Massachusetts, New Mexico, and North Carolina.

1950-51 After high school, traveled for eight months through the lower half of Africa painting watercolors. Traveled three months in Europe in 1951. Influenced by Notre Dame Cathedral. Wished to do leaded windows because of light.

1951-52 Whitney Art School in New Haven, Connecticut. Louis York, teacher.

1952-54 Drafted into U.S. Army. Stationed fourteen months in Korea. Painted murals at night; watercolors in spare time. On R & R in Japan, 1953, studied wood block printing and Japanese lacquer painting.

1954-56 Cranbrook Art Academy, Bloomfield Hills, Michigan. Majored in sculpture; did bronze casting, welding, stone, clay; minored in painting, metal smithing. Began to do commissions for leaded glass windows in buildings.

1956 First one-person show was in San Diego at Capri Theater. Jim Britton, curator.

1956-57 Hitch-hiked through Europe for eight months visiting cathedrals, friends in Italy, England, and France. Lived on farm in Spain for one month; painting and learning.

1958 ☐ Married Anne Stewart.
☐ Began building home, permanently moved to mountain site in Santa Ysabel, California in 1962. Compound and seven buildings completed by 1987. The work continues.
☐ Began working with Bruce Richards on most of his buildings in a rare art-and-architecture partnership which lasted until Richards's death in 1984. Did leaded windows, entry lighting fixtures, skylights, doors, carved columns, gardens, lights, railings, and gates.
☐ One person show at La Jolla Museum of Contemporary Art, La Jolla, California. Sculpture, plaster, and stained glass.

1960 ☐ Designed stained glass windows for St. Andrew's Episcopal Church, Pacific Beach, California.

1962 ☐ Worked on Wishing Well Hotel with Bruce Richards—Dining room (skylights, tables, entry doors, carved with leaded glass and wooden gates.
☐ Mixed media exhibition, Long Beach Museum, Long Beach, California.
☐ Sculpture in "California Design Seven," Pasadena Art Museum, Pasadena, California.
☐ Commissions: Resin/glass panel and hanging welded bronze sculpture for Cinema 21;

☐ Leaded glass windows for University Christian Church, San Diego, California.
☐ Building sculpture, welded copper, and interior lights for California Western College (now Pt. Loma Nazarene College), Pt. Loma, California.
☐ Doug Ring, first student apprentice, comes to work on Hubbell house.
☐ Playground sculptures for handicapped children—Sunshine Elementary School, San Diego, California.

1963 ☐ Sculpture—"California Design Eight," Pasadena Art Museum, Pasadena, California.

1964 ☐ Sculpture—Fine Arts Gallery, University of Nevada, Las Vegas, Nevada.
☐ Sculpture—The Sculpture Show, Dallas, Texas.

1965 ☐ Sculpture—Santa Barbara West Coast Sculpture Biennial, Santa Barbara, California.
☐ Selected large sculpture, leaded glass, and bronze sculpture—Pasadena Art Museum, Pasadena, California.
☐ Baptismal font and sculptures—St. Leo's Catholic Church, Solana Beach, California.
☐ Baptismal font, stations of the cross, tabernacle, and sculptures—St. Catherine Laboure Catholic Church, San Diego, California.

1967 ☐ Tabernacle—St. Francis College Seminary Chapel, San Diego, California.
☐ Memorial fountain—First Unitarian Church, San Diego, California.
☐ Award of Honor, American Institute of Architects, San Diego chapter, San Diego, California, for work in combining art and architecture.

1969 ☐ Leaded glass windows—San Diego Mission de Alcala, San Diego, California.
☐ Leaded glass windows—First Unity Church San Diego, California.
☐ One-person show, sculpture and stained glass—Miracosta College, Oceanside, California.

1970 ☐ Large leaded glass windows—All Souls Episcopal Church, Point Loma, California.

1972 ☐ Stained glass doors and windows—The Chart House Restaurant, Westwood, California.
☐ Outdoor theater and garden sculpture—Palomar College, San Diego, California.
☐ Design of Davidson Home, Alpine, California.
☐ Sculpture—The Founder's Gallery, University of San Diego, CA.

1973 ☐ Sanctuary, St. Alban's Episcopal Church, El Cajon, California.

☐ Outdoor meditation center and sundial—Spring Valley Presbyterian Church, Spring Valley, California.
☐ Restoration of an unfinished geodesic dome for use as a library and classrooms—Waldorf School, near Sacramento, California.
☐ Design concept and installation of Greenery Restaurant, Pacific Beach, California
☐ Stained glass entry doors and windows—The Chart House Restaurant, Point Loma, California.

1974 ☐ Sculpture of Angels and Our Lady of Guadalupe—San Diego Mission de Alcala, San Diego, California.
☐ Stained glass—Pacific Design Center, Los Angeles, California.
☐ Stained glass entry doors and windows—The Chart House Restaurant, La Jolla, California.

1975 ☐ Design concept and installation—Triton Restaurant, San Diego, California.

1976 ☐ Leaded glass—Yokohama Artists Exchange, Yokohama, Japan.
☐ Sculptures of eight saints and Father Serra—San Diego Mission de Alcala, San Diego, California.

1978 ☐ Tabernacle—Catholic Church of the Immaculata, San Diego University, San Diego, California.
☐ Main entrance facade—Vista Regional Center, San Diego County Courthouse, Vista, California.
☐ Twelve stained glass windows—Piedmont Community Church, Piedmont, California.
☐ Design concept and installation—Triton Restaurant (now Beach House), Cardiff, California.

1979 ☐ Davis Art Center, Davis, California. (Designed but never built)
☐ Design and installation—Antofte Stained Glass Workshop and Gallery, San Diego, California.

1980 ☐ One-person show of selected works—The San Diego County Board of Supervisors, San Diego, California.
■ "James Hubbell Day"–proclaimed by San Diego County Board of Supervisors and Public Arts Advisory committee, in conjunction with year-long program "San Diego County Honors the Seven Arts."

1981 ☐ Design and installation of eighteen leaded glass doors—Palace Doors, Abu Dhabi, United Arab Emirates, Saudi Arabia.
☐ Building Arts panel member, National Endowment for the Arts, Washington, DC.

1982 ☐ Ilan-Lael Foundation organized. Printed

five issues of "Hidden Leaves."
■ Award for Excellence in Landscape Design, American Society of Landscape Architects, for a residence in Rancho Santa Fe, California
☐ Bronze sculpture "Pegasus"—East County Performing Arts Center, El Cajon, California.
☐ One-person show, leaded glass—Gallery of New Glass, Scottsdale, Arizona.

1982-86 ☐ Six memorial stained glass windows—Vivian Webb Chapel, Webb School, Clairemont, California.

1982 ☐ Design of housing complex—Findhorn Community plan with Sim VanderRyn–Findhorn, Scotland. (not built).
☐ Designed carved doors and leaded glass windows—Findhorn Community Hall, Findhorn, Scotland.
☐ Outdoor sculpture of St. Elizabeth Sexton—University of San Diego, San Diego, California.

1983-84 ☐ Design of Vint Residence, Del Mar, California.

1983 ☐ One-person show, sculpture, watercolors, and stained glass—Felicita Foundation, Escondido, California.

1984 ☐ Design of Meditation Chapel, Sea Ranch, California, including interior furnishings.
☐ One-person show, drawings, sculpture, and watercolors—Friends of Jung Center, San Diego, California.

1984 ■ Special Award, A.I.A., San Diego chapter, with Kay Kaiser, for promoting better design and planning through *Hidden Leaves* magazine.

1985 ■ Excellence in Craftsmanship Award, California State A.I.A., for Sea Ranch Chapel.
☐ Memorial sculpture—Santa Ysabel Indian Mission, Santa Ysabel, California.
☐ Doors, leaded glass windows, and fireplace—Rancho La Puerta, Tecate, Mexico.
☐ Architectural design—International Gallery and New School of Architecture, San Diego, California.

1986 ■ Gold Nugget Award, Pacific Coast Builders Conference, San Francisco, California, for Sea Ranch Chapel, Sea Ranch, California.

1987 ■ Citation Award for excellence in design for the Sea Ranch Chapel—I.F.R.A.A., (Interfaith Forum on Religion, Art, and Architecture), an A.I.A. affiliate.
☐ Interior design, mural, and sculpture—St. Alban's Episcopal Church, El Cajon, California.
☐ Doors, windows, and mosaic—Camp Stevens, Episcopal Church Camp, Julian, California.

1988 ☐ Mosaic sculptured walls and mural for lobby renovation—Alvarado Hospital, San Diego, California.
☐ One-person show—Athenaeum Art Library, La Jolla, California.
☐ One-person show, watercolors, iron and bronze sculptures—Philip Bareiss Fine Arts, Taos, New Mexico.
☐ Bronze fountain—Trinity Episcopal Church, Escondido, California.

1989 ☐ KPBS Television special and video—"The Art and Vision of James Hubbell."
■ "James Hubbell Day"–proclaimed by San Diego County Board of Supervisors and Public Arts Advisory committee.

1990-97 ☐ Annual lectures and workshops—San Francisco Institute of Architecture.
☐ Design of two schools—Colonia de Esperanza, Tijuana, Mexico.

1990 ☐ Soil and Soul Design/Build Workshop with Milenko Matanovic—Kuchumaa Chapel, Rancho La Puerta, Tecate, Mexico.
☐ Artists Exchange and Art Show, Vladivostok, Russia.
☐ Design of small interior employee chapel—Catholic Charity Center, S.H.A.R.E., San Diego, California.
☐ Building design—Guest House, La Jolla, California.

1991 ☐ Lecture on "Organic Architecture" and student workshop—University of North Carolina, Charlotte, North Carolina.
☐ Design and building of Gay Residence, Julian, California.
☐ One-person show—Athenaeum Art Library, La Jolla, California.
☐ Workshop—Omega Institute of Holistic Studies, Rhinebeck, New York.

1992 ☐ Lecture on "Organic Architecture"—University of California Berkeley.

1992-1996 ☐ Annual, hands-on La Rosa Blanca Workshop, Tijuana, Mexico, and Julian, California.

1993 ☐ Lectures and workshops—Institute of Architecture, San Francisco, California.
☐ Volunteer Workshop to build entrance—Volcan Mountain Preserve, Julian, California.
☐ Lecture and workshop, "Organic Architecture"—University of Maine at Augusta.
☐ Lecture on "Continuous Architecture."—Smithsonian Institution, Washington D.C.
☐ Leaded glass windows—Good Samaritan Episcopal Church, La Jolla, California.
■ Citation Award for excellence in design for the Sea Ranch Chapel—I.F.R.A.A., (Interfaith Forum on Religion, Art, and Architecture), an A.I.A. affiliate

1994 ☐ One-person show—Santa Ysabel Art Gallery, Santa Ysabel, California.
☐ Soil and Soul Design/Build Workshop with Milenko Matanovic—Far Eastern State Technical University, Vladivostok, Russia, Created an amphitheater/park.
■ Named honorary Professor—Far Eastern State Technical University, Vladivostok, Russia.
■ C-3 Revelle Award for lifetime dedication to the arts, environment, and urban planning.

1995 ☐ Steel sculpture—Crest Corporate Center, City of Escondido, California
☐ Design and park layout—Pickering Park and Amphitheater, Issaquah, Washington.
☐ Workshop with Milenko Matanovic—Omega Institute of Holistic Studies, Rhinebeck, New York.
☐ Workshop—Yestermorrow Design/Build School, Warren, Vermont.
☐ Lecture—Institute of Contemporary Arts, London, England.
☐ Lecture—Royal Institute of Architecture, London, England.
☐ Lecture—Catholic Church National Art & Architecture, Form & Reform Conference, San Diego, California.
☐ Lecture—Community Built Association Conference, Malibu, California.
☐ Installed gate, completed park—Soil and Soul Design/Build Workshop, Far Eastern State Technical University, Vladivostok, Russia.
☐ Designed underwater concept house with son Drew—Deep Dream, La Jolla, California.
☐ One-person show—Santa Ysabel Art Gallery, Santa Ysabel, California.
☐ Lecture—Catholic Church National Art & Architecture, Form and Reform, San Diego, California.
☐ One-person show—Trios Gallery, Solana Beach, California.

1996 ☐ Lecture—Cal Poly, San Luis Obispo, California.
☐ Designed Beaton Residence, Jamul, California.
☐ Bench, fountain, and sculpture—Quail Botanical Gardens, Encinitas, California.
☐ One person show—Santa Ysabel Art Gallery, Santa Ysabel, California.
☐ Workshop—Yestermorrow Design/Build School, Warren, Vermont.

1997 ☐ Lecture—Community Built Association Conference, Oceanside, California.
☐ One-person show—Santa Ysabel Art Gallery, Santa Ysabel, California.
☐ One-person show, watercolors—La Jolla Artists Gallery, La Jolla, CA.
☐ Design of guest house—Orcas Island, Washington.
■ Special award—International Visitor Council.
■ Orchid Award—San Diego Chapter AIA–for work at Camp Stevens, California.
☐ Began plans for city park, Cincinnati, Ohio.
☐ Four doors for Tecate—Children's environmental center.

BOOKS AND PERIODICALS *(Partial List)*

Alan Hess, *Hyperwest: American Residential Architecture on the Edge*, Whitney Library of Design, New York, NY, 1996. pp. 30-33

James and Roberta Swan, *Dialogues with Living Earth*, Quest Books, Wheaton, Illinois, 1996, p. 258

Patty Jo Cornish, *An Outrageous Idea: Natural Prayer*, Illustrated by James Hubbell, Hilltop House Publishers, San Diego, California, 1996

Mark Dudek, *Kindergarten Architecture: Space for the Imagination*, E & FN Spon, London, England, 1996, p. 140

James Hubbell, "Building Architecture Towards Community" *Friends of Kebyar*, Vol. 14 Issue #60; September 1995 through June 1996, p. 12

Milenko Matanovic, *Lightworks,* Lorian Press, Issaquah, Washington, 1995, p. 15

David Pearson, *Earth To Spirit, In Search of Natural Architecture*, Gaia Books Ltd., London, 1994, p. 67

Kim Ostler, "Organic Chemistry in California," *World Architecture,* Issue 30, The Independent Magazine of the International Academy of Architecture, 1994, p. 62

Claudia Carlin, "Jardin de Ninos, Beyond Borders," *Mexico! Business and Life*, Volume I, No. 2, 1994, p.12

Brenda Belfield (coordinator), *Faith and Form*, Journal of the Interfaith Forum on Religion, Art and Architecture, Vol. XXVII Winter 1993-94, p. 26

David Graham, "Spirited Designs," *Westways Magazine*, October, 1994, pg. 8

James Hubbell, *Earthword*, The Journal of Environmental and Social Responsibility, Issue #5, 1994, p. 44

Debra Lee Baldwin, "Over The Rainbow," *San Diego Union, Homescape Extra*, April 15, 1994, p. 12

Editorial, *Organic Architecture*, Architectural Design Profile No. 106, 1993, p. 88

Sally Woodbridge, "Sea Ranch Meditation Chapel, Things in Motion" *Progressive Architecture*, June, 1992, cover and p. 74

James Hubbell, *To Walk the Emerald Gate*, Collection of poems and drawings, self-published, 1992

Laurence McMillin, *Encounters With Individual Humanities*, Illustrations by James Hubbell, The Webb Schools, Claremont, California, 1991

Barbara Moran, "A Home From Sculptor's Hands," *Los Angeles Times*, January 26, 1991. p. 1, Section K

Timothy Carpenter, "Sea Ranch Chapel: Coaxing Wood, Copper, and Shingles Into Sculpture," *Fine Home Building*, Issue #64, January 1991, p. 50

James Hubbell, "Rainbow Hill," *Fine Home Building*, Annual Issue of Homes Spring, #66, 1991, p. 51

Horst Rasch, "Das Gegehstuck Zum Schuhkarton," *Schoner Wohnen*, April 4, 1990, p. 48

Horst Rasch, "Motstykket Til Margarinkasser," Maison NR 3, July 1990, p. 76

Kay Kaiser, "Hubbell's World," *KPBS On Air*, April l989, p. 22

Julie Sinclair Eakin, "California Dreamin'," *Diversion Magazine*, May 1989, p. 241

Brindle Miller, "Fountain of Art," *Times Advocate Quarterly*, Vol. II, No. 1, March 1989, p. 41

James Hubbell, *Is There Life After 50 For a Middle-Aged Hat?* Humorous story, self-published, 1988.

Phyllis Van Doren, "From The Palm of His Hand," *San Diego Home and Garden*, November 1988, p. 54

Robert Perine, I. Andrea, Bram Dijkstra, *San Diego Artists*, "James Hubbell," Artra Publishing, Encinitas, California, 1988, p. 116

Editorial, "Wenn Die Form Zum Ornament Wird . . ." *Architektur und Technik*; September 1987, p. 6

Jack Golden, "The Vision is a Song," *Friends of Kebyar—Special Edition*, Vol. 5.2, Issue #33, February-April 1987.

Editorial, A+U (*Architecture & Urbanism*), No. 174, March 1985, p. 86, 87

Clare White, "Fantasy Land," *San Diego Magazine*, August 1984, p. 118

Carmel Repp, *So You Want To Design?* Environmental Design for Children, Illustrated by James Hubbell, March 21, 1983.

Otto Rigan, "The Making of the Palace Doors," *Glass Studio*; No. 34, 1982, p. 26

Otto Rigan, "James Hubbell: A Visionary's World" *Glass Studio*, No. 30, 1982, p. 30

Otto Rigan, *The Palace Doors of Abu Dhabi*, Hidden House Publications, Palo Alto, California and Putnam Publishing Company, New York, 1982

Matthias Wendt, "Optische Stimulation Der Umwelt," *Color Foto Magazine*, February 1981, p. 68

Zenia Cleigh, "Paradise Found," *San Diego Magazine*, Februray 1979, p. 102

Otto Rigan, *From The Earth Up*, McGraw-Hill, New York, 1979.

Wolfgang M. Ebert, *Home Sweet Dome*, Verlag Dieter Fricke, Frankfurt-Main, Germany, 1978, p. 77

Jim Higgs and Charles Milligan, *The Wizard's Eye*, Chronicle Books, San Francisco, 1978. p. 28

Art Boericke and Barry Shapiro, *The Craftsman Builder*, Simon and Schuster, New York, 1977.

Eudora Moore, Craftsman Lifestyle–*The Gentle Revolution*, California Design Publications, Pasadena, California, 1977, p. 12

Otto Rigan, *New Glass*, San Francisco Book Co., 1976; paperback, Ballantine Press, 1977 p. 82, 111

James Hubbell, *Love Letters To The Earth*, self-published poetry, 1975. Russian translation, 1990.

Gilbert M. Grosvenor, *The Craftsman in America*, National Geographic Society, 1975, p. 176

Oberto Gili and Norma Skurka, *Underground Interiors*, Quadrangle Books, New York, NY, 1972, p. 48

Don MacMasters, "Pools: An Affair of the Heart," *Los Angeles Times*, Home Section, April 16, 1972, p. 16

Don MacMasters, "A Sculptor's House," *Los Angeles Times*, Home Section, March 24, 1968, p. 16

James DeLong, "Fantasy House Down to Earth," *House Beautiful*, June, 1967, p. 118

VIDEOS

1996   "Soil and Earth Park–Soil and Soul Workshop" in Vladivostok, Russia. Produced by Vivian Blackstone.

1996   "Ninos de Esperanza (Children of Hope)" by Brennan Hubbell and Paul Carlson. Documentary about the building of the kindergarten and elementary school in Tijuana, Mexico designed by James T. Hubbell.

1990   "You Are The Miracle!"–The secrets of James Hubbell, Beatrice Wood, Al Struckus, Vivika and Otto Heino to enrich your life and find your creative magic. Produced By Andrea Simmons.

1989   "Kuchumaa Passage"–Apprentice Workshop "Soil and Soul," Produced by Peli-Graphic Productions, Tecate, Mexico

1989   "The Art and Vision of James Hubbell," Television special produced by Paul Marshall and Vernon Kifer, KPBS San Diego.